Microsoft®
Word 2010:
Level 1 of 3

JUDY MARDAR
PC Source

PAMELA R. TOLIVER
Soft-Spec

LABYRINTH
LEARNING™

El Sobrante, CA

Microsoft Word 2010: Level 1
by Judy Mardar and Pamela R. Toliver

Copyright © 2011 by Labyrinth Learning

Labyrinth Learning
P.O. Box 20818
El Sobrante, California 24820
800.522.9746
On the web at lablearning.com

President:
Brian Favro

Product Development Manager:
Jason Favro

Managing Editor:
Laura A. Lionello

Production Manager:
Rad Proctor

eLearning Production Manager:
Arl S. Nadel

Editorial/Production Team:
Donna Bacidore, John Barlow,
Scott Benjamin, Belinda Breyer, Alec Fehl,
Sandy Jones, PMG Media

Indexing: Joanne Sprott

Interior Design:
Mark Ong, Side-by-Side Studios

Cover Design:
Words At Work

ITEM: 1-59136-307-1
ISBN-13: 978-1-59136-307-1

Manufactured in the United States of America.

10 9 8 7 6 5 4 3 2

Table of Contents

LESSON 5: WORKING WITH TABLES AND FORMS 162

Quick Reference Tables

Preface

Microsoft® Word 2010: Level 1 provides thorough training of Word 2010 introductory skills. This course is supported with comprehensive instructor resources and our eLab assessment and learning management tool. And, our new work-readiness exercises ensure students have the critical thinking skills necessary to succeed to today's world. After completing this course, students will be able to successfully face the challenges presented in the next book in this series, *Microsoft Word 2010: Level 2*.

Visual Conventions

This book uses many visual and typographic cues to guide students through the lessons. This page provides examples and describes the function of each cue.

Type this text   Anything you should type at the keyboard is printed in this typeface.

    Tips, Notes, and Warnings are used throughout the text to draw attention to certain topics.

Command→
Command→
Command, etc.   This convention indicates how to give a command from the Ribbon. The commands are written: Ribbon Tab→Command Group→Command→Subcommand.

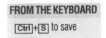   These margin notes indicate shortcut keys for executing a task described in the text.

Exercise Progression

The exercises in this book build in complexity as students work through a lesson toward mastery of the skills taught.

- **Develop Your Skills** exercises are introduced immediately after concept discussions. They provide detailed, step-by-step tutorials.
- **Reinforce Your Skills** exercises provide additional hands-on practice with moderate assistance.
- **Apply Your Skills** exercises test students' skills by describing the correct results without providing specific instructions on how to achieve them.
- **Critical Thinking and Work-Readiness Skills** exercises are the most challenging. They provide generic instructions, allowing students to use their skills and creativity to achieve the results they envision.

Working with Word Basics

LEARNING OBJECTIVES

After studying this lesson, you will be able to:

- Use and customize the Ribbon
- Use the Quick Access toolbar and the Mini toolbar
- Open and close documents
- Navigate in a document
- Use Word Help

In this lesson, you will get an overview of Microsoft Office Word 2010. First you will learn to start Word, and then how to work with the Word interface. You will open and close documents, navigate through a multipage document, and work with Word Help. Finally, you will exit the Word program.

Getting Oriented to Word 2010

My Virtual Campus

Stefanie Bentley has been promoted to marketing assistant at My Virtual Campus, a social networking technology company. My Virtual Campus sells their web application to colleges and universities, allowing students, alumni, faculty, and staff to utilize this social networking website, which is closed to the public and branded for their institution. Her first task is to create a brief summary of what their best-selling website is and how it is used. This effort will provide Stefanie a good opportunity to see just how easy Microsoft Word 2010 is to use when writing her paper, and if she runs into any problems along the way, she will appreciate how much help is at her fingertips.

My Virtual Campus

Our best-selling website, a social networking Intranet established specifically for college communities worldwide, has been gaining popularity at an extraordinary rate.

The website is useful for all types of networking opportunities; for example, social events and career prospects can be publicized, prospective students can check out the campus, professors and students can participate in extended training occasions and collaborate on special projects. It also proves useful when looking for a roommate or offering items for sale. Alumni can post job opportunities for current students and other noteworthy news, and so forth.

In general, here's how it works; you join and create a profile about yourself, choosing how much personal information to enter. Then, you can invite other people to join also. You can chat in real-time with other members, post photos to share, and most importantly, you can control what information others can see about you.

Security is taken very seriously by My Virtual Campus and every step has been taken to ensure your privacy and protect your confidential information.

1.1 Presenting Word 2010

Video Lesson   labyrinthelab.com/videos

Microsoft Office Word 2010 is a dynamic document-authoring program that lets you create and easily modify a variety of documents. Word provides tools to assist you in virtually every aspect of document creation. From desktop publishing to web publishing, Word has the right tool for the job. For these and many other reasons, Word is the most widely used word processing program in homes and businesses.

1.2 Starting Word

The method you use to start Word depends on whether you intend to create a new document or open an existing one. If you intend to create a new document, use one of the following methods to start Word:

- Click the ⊕ button, choose Microsoft Office from the All Programs menu, and then choose Microsoft Word 2010.
- Click the Microsoft Word 2010 ⊞ button on the Quick Launch toolbar located at the left edge of the taskbar. (This button may not appear on all computers.)

Use one of the following methods if you intend to open an existing Word document. Once the Word program starts, the desired document will open in a Word window.

- Navigate to the desired document using Windows Explorer or My Computer and double-click the document name.
- Click the ⊕ button and choose Documents. Choose Recently Changed under Favorites, and then double-click the desired document name.

After you start Word, the document window shows. Don't be concerned if your document window looks a little different from this example. The Word screen is customizable.

File tab—This tab leads to file management tasks, including opening, printing, and saving your work. The File tab also leads to Backstage view, which provides information about the document and options to change Word's default settings.

Quick Access toolbar—Frequently used commands appear here, and you can add your own favorites.

The Ribbon—This is control central, where you find the tools you need to build, format, and edit your documents.

Title bar—The name of your document appears here. You see a generic *Documentx* name until you save and name your document.

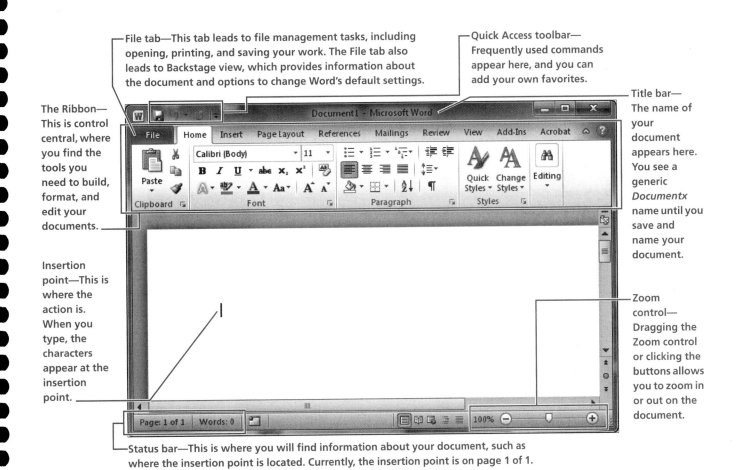

Insertion point—This is where the action is. When you type, the characters appear at the insertion point.

Zoom control—Dragging the Zoom control or clicking the buttons allows you to zoom in or out on the document.

Status bar—This is where you will find information about your document, such as where the insertion point is located. Currently, the insertion point is on page 1 of 1.

The insertion point is sometimes referred to as the cursor.

Start Word

In this exercise, you will experience starting Word, and you will examine the Word window.

1. If necessary, **start** your computer. The Windows Desktop appears.
2. **Click** the ⬤ button at the left edge of the taskbar, and choose **All Programs**.
3. Choose **Microsoft Office→Microsoft Word 2010** from the menu.
4. Make sure the Word window is **maximized** ▣.

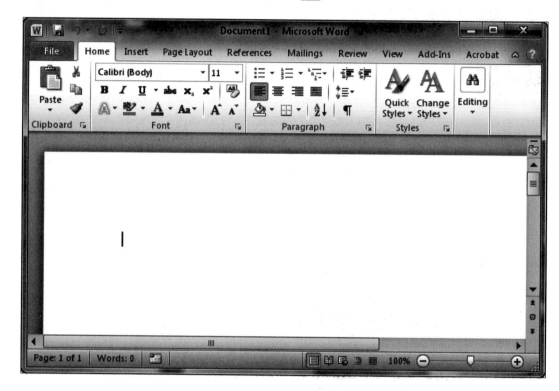

1.3 Opening Documents

Video Lesson labyrinthelab.com/videos

The Open command on the File tab displays the Open dialog box, where you can navigate to a storage location and open previously saved documents. Once a document is open, you can edit or print it.

Opening Older Word Documents

If you open a document created in a previous version of Word, 2007 and earlier, it opens in Compatibility Mode. The term appears in the Title bar, as shown in the illustration. Older Word documents do not understand the new features in Word 2010, so those features are limited or disabled.

 When an older document is open, a Convert command is available in Backstage view, which you can use to upgrade the file and make the new features of Word 2010 available.

Storing Your Exercise Files

Throughout this book, you will be referred to files in your "file storage location." You can store your exercise files on various media, such as on a USB flash drive, in the Documents folder, or to a network drive at a school or company. While some figures may display files on a USB flash drive, it is assumed that you will substitute your own location for that shown in the figures. See Storing Your Exercise Files for additional information on alternative storage media. Storing Your Exercise Files is available on the student web page for this book at labpub.com/learn/word10/.

 In Windows XP, the folder is called My Documents. In Windows Vista and Windows 7, it is called Documents. Throughout this book we will use the word Documents when referring to this folder.

If you have not yet copied the student exercise files to your local file storage location, follow the instructions in Storing Your Exercise Files, located on the student web page for this book.

Open a Document

In this exercise, you will learn the steps to open an existing document through the Open dialog box.

Before You Begin: Navigate to the student web page for this book at labpub.com/learn/word10 and see the Downloading the Student Exercise Files section of Storing Your Exercise Files for instructions on how to retrieve the student exercise files for this book and to copy them to your file storage location.

1. Follow these steps to open the document:

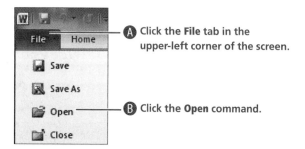

Ⓐ Click the **File** tab in the upper-left corner of the screen.

Ⓑ Click the **Open** command.

 Later in this lesson, the preceding steps will be written like this: Click the File (or File) tab and choose Open from the menu.

2. When the **Open** dialog box appears, follow these steps to open the My Virtual Campus document:

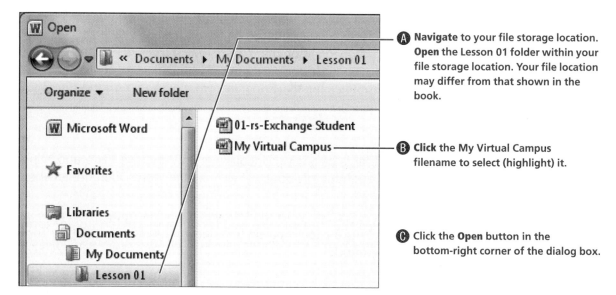

Ⓐ **Navigate** to your file storage location. **Open** the Lesson 01 folder within your file storage location. Your file location may differ from that shown in the book.

Ⓑ **Click** the My Virtual Campus filename to select (highlight) it.

Ⓒ Click the **Open** button in the bottom-right corner of the dialog box.

 You can also double-click on a filename to open it.

3. Make sure the Word window is **maximized** 🔲.

1.4 Working with the Word 2010 Interface

Video Lesson   labyrinthelab.com/videos

The band running across the top of the screen is the Ribbon. This is where you will find the tools for building, formatting, and editing your documents. You can customize the Ribbon by adding new tabs with their own groups and commands.

The Ribbon

The Ribbon consists of three primary areas: tabs, groups, and commands. The tabs include Home, Insert, Page Layout, and so on. A group houses related commands within a tab. Groups on the Home tab, for instance, include Clipboard, Font, Paragraph, Styles, and Editing. An example of a command in the Paragraph group is Increase Indent.

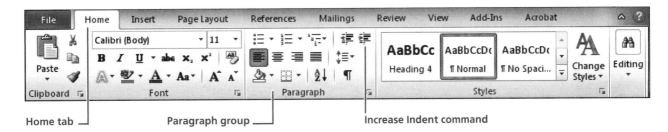

Home tab _| Paragraph group _| Increase Indent command

Be aware that the arrangement of the buttons on the Ribbon can vary, depending on your screen resolution and how the Word window is sized. Following are two examples of how the Paragraph group might appear on the Ribbon.

Contextual Tabs

Contextual tabs appear in context with the task you are performing. As shown in the following illustration, double-clicking a clip art object in a document activates Picture Tools, with the Format tab in the foreground.

 You have to double-click the object the first time to activate the contextual tab; afterward, you only have to click the object once to reactivate it.

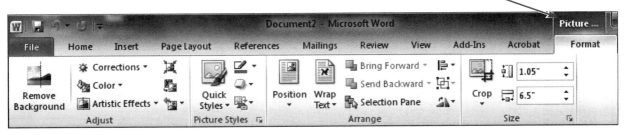

Dialog Box Launcher

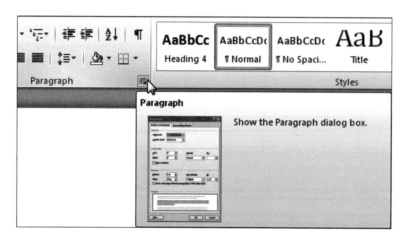 Some groups include a dialog box launcher in the bottom-right corner of the group. This means that there are additional commands available for the group. Clicking the launcher opens the dialog box, or it may open a task pane, which, like a dialog box, houses additional commands related to the group.

The dialog box launcher displays the dialog box or task pane available for a given command.

Live Preview with Galleries

Live Preview shows what a formatting change looks like without actually applying the format. In the following example, selecting a block of text, and then hovering the mouse pointer over a font in the font gallery, previews how the text will look. Clicking the font name applies the font to the text.

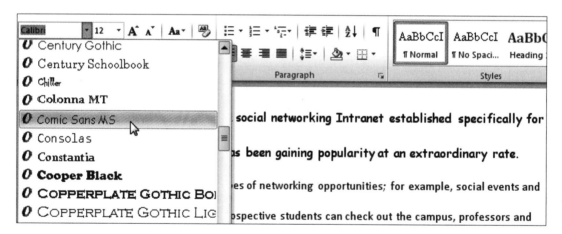

Live Preview of the Comic Sans MS Font

Hide the Ribbon

If you want more room to work, you can temporarily hide the Ribbon by double-clicking the active tab. This collapses the Ribbon, as shown in the following illustration.

Clicking a tab, such as Home, redisplays the full Ribbon temporarily. It collapses again when you click in the document. If you want the Ribbon to remain open, double-click the same tab you used to collapse it, or right-click on the Ribbon and choose Minimize the Ribbon to turn off the feature.

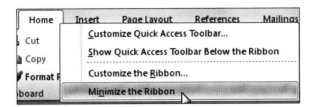

Customize the Ribbon

The Ribbon can now be customized, making it easier for you to have access to the commands that you use frequently all under one tab, if you like. You can add new groups to existing tabs or add new tabs with their own groups and commands. You can always restore the original Ribbon tabs, groups, and commands very easily.

You cannot add new commands to an existing group on the original Ribbon.

When you choose to add a new tab to the Ribbon, the new tab appears on the right of the active tab; however, you can move it at any time. The new tab includes an empty new group, ready for you to add commands to it. You use the Move Up and Move Down arrows in the Word Options dialog box to reposition existing tabs and groups.

Move Up and Move Down arrows

DEVELOP YOUR SKILLS 1.4.1

Work with the Ribbon

In this exercise, you will explore the various aspects of the Ribbon, including tabs, contextual tabs, the dialog box launcher, and Live Preview. Finally, you'll hide and unhide the Ribbon, and learn how to customize it.

Display the Insert Tab

1. Click the **Insert** tab on the Ribbon to display the commands available in that category.

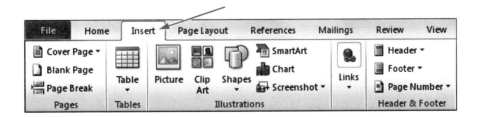

2. Take a moment to investigate some of the other tabs on the Ribbon, and then return to the **Home** tab.

Display Contextual Tabs and Use the Dialog Box Launcher

3. **Double-click** the clip art object at the top of your document to display Picture Tools on the Ribbon.

Selection handles (small circles and squares) surround an object when you click it.

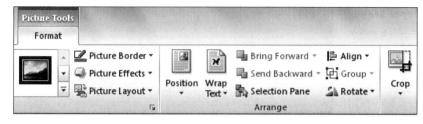

Picture Tools

4. Click anywhere in the **document** to deselect the clip art.

5. Hover the **mouse pointer** over the dialog box launcher in the bottom-right corner of the Font group to display the ToolTip, as shown here.

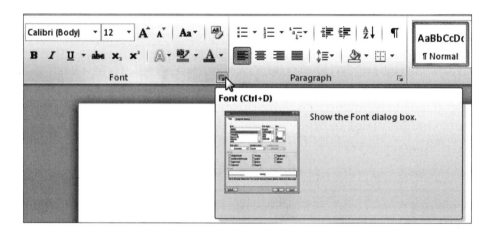

6. Click the **dialog box launcher** to open the Font dialog box.

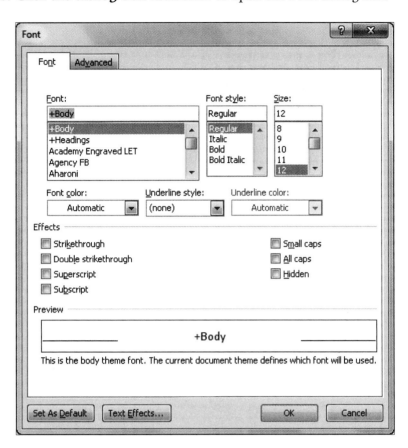

This dialog box provides additional tools for formatting text.

7. Click the **Cancel** button in the bottom-right corner to close the dialog box.

Use Live Preview

8. Position the **mouse pointer** in the white, left margin area of the second paragraph. Then, **double-click** the left mouse button to select (highlight) the entire paragraph, as shown here.
If you notice a little toolbar fade in, you can ignore it for now. It will fade away on its own.

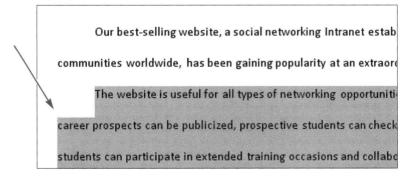

9. Follow these steps to use Live Preview:

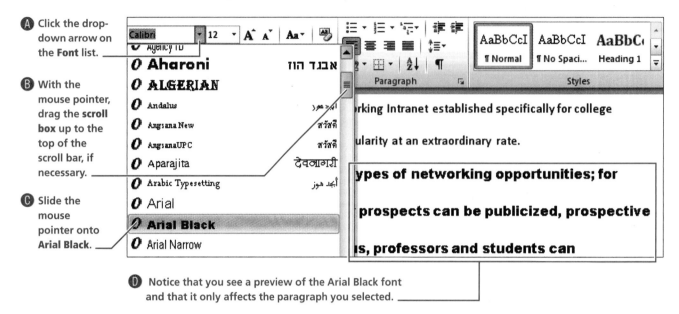

Ⓐ Click the drop-down arrow on the **Font** list.

Ⓑ With the mouse pointer, drag the **scroll box** up to the top of the scroll bar, if necessary.

Ⓒ Slide the mouse pointer onto **Arial Black.**

Ⓓ Notice that you see a preview of the Arial Black font and that it only affects the paragraph you selected.

10. Take a moment to **preview** a few other fonts.

11. Click anywhere in the document to close the font list, and **click** once again to deselect the highlighted text.

Minimize/Restore the Ribbon

12. Double-click the Home tab to minimize the Ribbon.

13. Right-click a Ribbon tab and choose **Minimize the Ribbon** from the menu to turn off the feature.

Add a New Tab to the Ribbon

14. **Right-click** the Home tab and then choose **Customize the Ribbon**.

15. Follow these steps to add a new tab to the Ribbon:

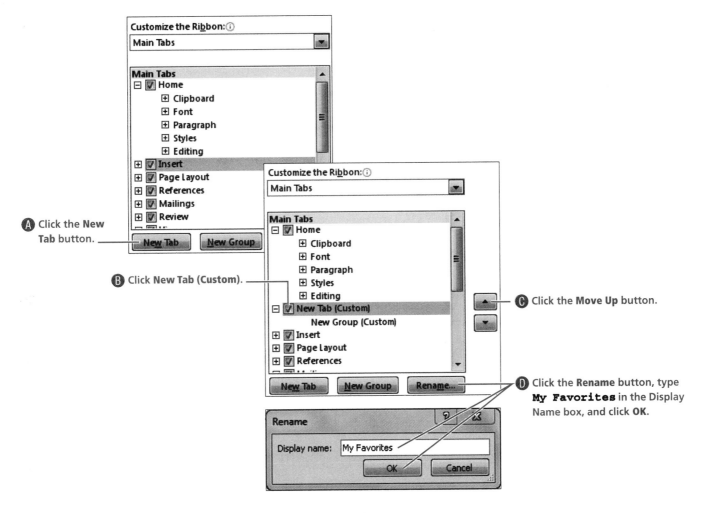

Ⓐ Click the **New Tab** button.

Ⓑ Click **New Tab (Custom)**.

Ⓒ Click the **Move Up** button.

Ⓓ Click the **Rename** button, type **My Favorites** in the Display Name box, and click **OK**.

Notice when you create a new tab, it automatically includes a new group for you to customize with commands.

16. Click **OK** again in the Word Options dialog box, and then click the new **My Favorites** tab. *Notice the new tab is to the left of the Home tab, there are currently no commands on the new tab, and there is a blank New Group awaiting commands to be added to it.*

Add a New Group to the My Favorites Tab

17. **Right-click** the My Favorites tab and choose **Customize the Ribbon**.

18. Follow these steps to add a new group:

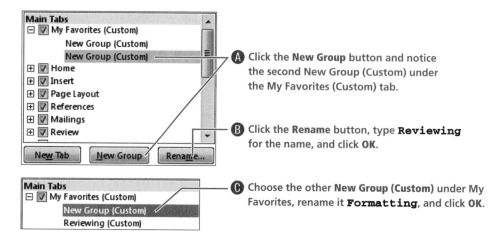

Leave the Word Options box open so you can add commands to your new groups.

Add Commands to Custom Groups

19. If necessary, click the **Formatting (Custom)** group.

20. Follow these steps to add commands to the group:

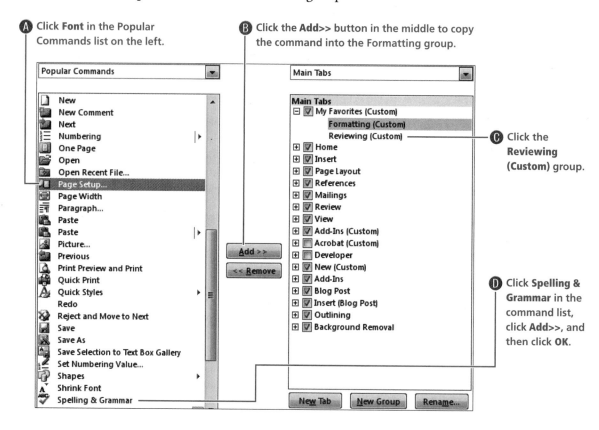

Notice the Ribbon now has a new tab named My Favorites that contains two new groups, Formatting and Reviewing, each containing one command.

Restore the Original Ribbon

21. **Right-click** the Home tab and choose **Customize the Ribbon**.

22. Follow these steps to delete the tab, groups, and commands you made earlier:

Ⓐ Click the **Reset** button.

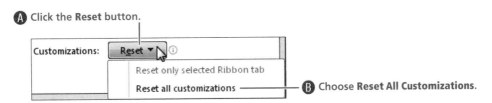

Ⓑ Choose **Reset All Customizations**.

23. Click **Yes** in the message box confirming the action, and then click **OK**.

The Quick Access Toolbar

Video Lesson   labyrinthelab.com/videos

The Quick Access toolbar in the upper-left corner of the screen contains frequently used commands. It is customizable and operates independently from the Ribbon.

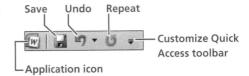

Moving the Quick Access Toolbar

You can place the Quick Access toolbar in one of two positions on the screen. The default position is in the upper-left corner. Clicking the Customize Quick Access toolbar button at the right edge of the toolbar reveals a menu from which you can choose Show Below the Ribbon.

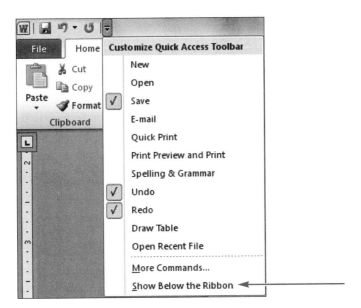

The Customize Quick Access Toolbar menu conveniently lists a series of frequently used commands that you can add to the toolbar by choosing them from the menu.

Customizing the Quick Access Toolbar

You can add buttons to and remove them from the Quick Access toolbar to suit your needs. You might want to add commands you use regularly so they are always available.

Right-click the Ribbon command you want to add (Center in this example), and choose Add to Quick Access Toolbar from the shortcut menu.

 The terms shortcut, context, pop-up, and drop-down are used interchangeably when referring to a secondary menu that appears.

To remove a button from the Quick Access toolbar, right-click the button and choose Remove from Quick Access Toolbar from the shortcut menu.

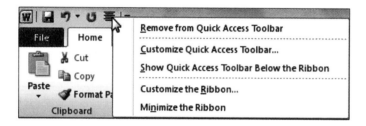

QUICK REFERENCE	WORKING WITH THE QUICK ACCESS TOOLBAR
Task	**Procedure**
Add a button to the toolbar	▪ Right-click the button you want to add. ▪ Choose Add to Quick Access Toolbar from the menu.
Remove a button from the toolbar	▪ Right-click the button you want to remove. ▪ Choose Remove from Quick Access Toolbar from the shortcut menu.
Change the location of the toolbar	▪ Click the Customize Quick Access Toolbar button at the right edge of the toolbar. ▪ Choose Show Below (or Above) the Ribbon.

Work with the Quick Access Toolbar

In this exercise, you will reposition the Quick Access toolbar, and then you will customize it by adding and removing buttons.

Change the Quick Access Toolbar Location

1. Follow these steps to move the Quick Access toolbar below the Ribbon:

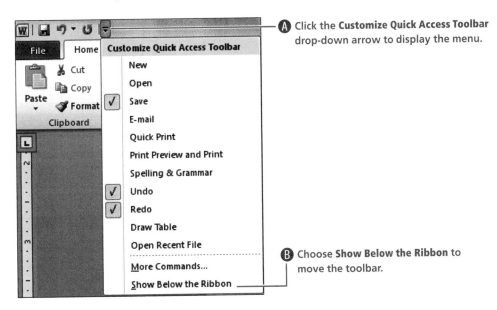

Ⓐ Click the **Customize Quick Access Toolbar** drop-down arrow to display the menu.

Ⓑ Choose **Show Below the Ribbon** to move the toolbar.

The toolbar appears below the Ribbon at the left edge of the window. Now you will return it to its original position.

2. Click the **drop-down arrow** at the right edge of the Quick Access toolbar again, and this time choose **Show Above the Ribbon**.

Add a Button to the Quick Access Toolbar

3. Make sure that the **Home** tab is active, and then follow these steps to add the Bullets button to the toolbar:

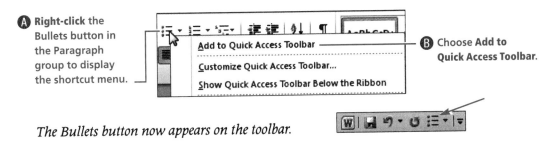

Ⓐ **Right-click** the Bullets button in the Paragraph group to display the shortcut menu.

Ⓑ Choose **Add to Quick Access Toolbar.**

The Bullets button now appears on the toolbar.

Remove a Button from the Quick Access Toolbar

4. **Right-click** the Bullets button on the Quick Access toolbar and choose the **Remove from Quick Access Toolbar** command.

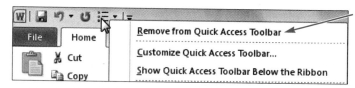

The button disappears from the Quick Access toolbar.

The Mini Toolbar

Video Lesson labyrinthelab.com/videos

There's another toolbar in Word, and it contains frequently used formatting commands. When you select (highlight) text, the Mini toolbar fades in. After a pause, it fades away. Make it reappear by right-clicking the selected text.

In the following example, clicking the Bold **B** button on the Mini toolbar applies the Bold feature to the selected text.

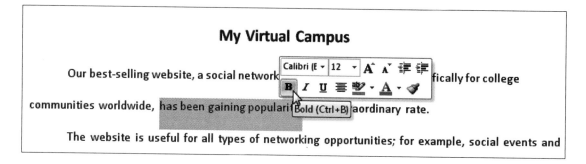

DEVELOP YOUR SKILLS 1.4.3
Use the Mini Toolbar

In this exercise, you will use the Mini toolbar to format text.

1. Follow these steps to italicize a paragraph:

Ⓐ Position the **mouse pointer** in the white margin to the left of the first paragraph and then **double-click** to select (highlight) the paragraph.

Ⓑ When the Mini toolbar fades in, click the **Italic** button.

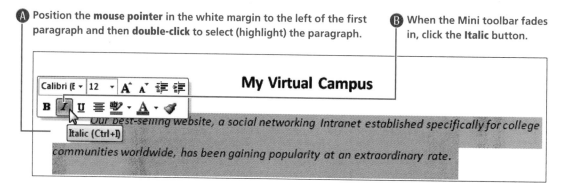

If this timid little toolbar disappears, right-click the highlighted text and it will reappear.

2. **Click** anywhere in the document to deselect the text and view the formatted paragraph.

3. Select the **first paragraph** again and click the **Italic** button to remove the formatting.

1.5 Navigating in a Word Document

Video Lesson   labyrinthelab.com/videos

If you are working in a multipage document, it is helpful to know about various techniques for moving through a document. You can navigate using the scroll bar located at the right side of the screen, or you can use keystrokes.

Navigating with the Scroll Bar

The scroll bar lets you browse through documents; however, it does not move the insertion point. After scrolling, you must click in the document where you want to reposition the insertion point. The following illustration shows the components of the scroll bar.

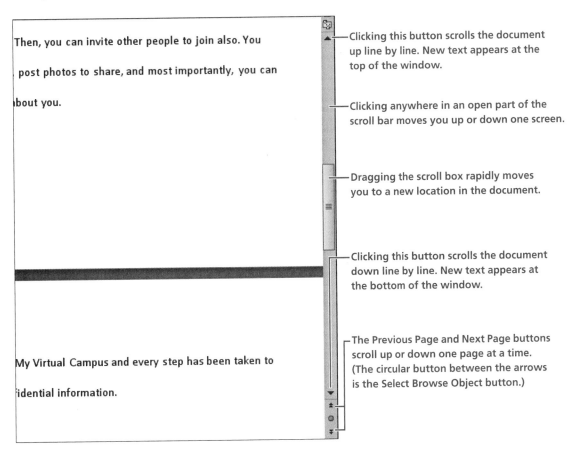

Then, you can invite other people to join also. You

post photos to share, and most importantly, you can

bout you.

Clicking this button scrolls the document up line by line. New text appears at the top of the window.

Clicking anywhere in an open part of the scroll bar moves you up or down one screen.

Dragging the scroll box rapidly moves you to a new location in the document.

Clicking this button scrolls the document down line by line. New text appears at the bottom of the window.

My Virtual Campus and every step has been taken to

idential information.

The Previous Page and Next Page buttons scroll up or down one page at a time. (The circular button between the arrows is the Select Browse Object button.)

Positioning the Insertion Point

When the mouse pointer is in a text area, it resembles an uppercase "I" and it is referred to as an I-beam. The insertion point is positioned at the location where you click the I-beam and it begins flashing. Thus, wherever the insertion point is flashing, that is where the action begins.

DEVELOP YOUR SKILLS 1.5.1

Practice Scrolling and Positioning the Insertion Point

In this exercise, you will use the scroll bar to practice moving through a document, and then you will position the insertion point.

Scroll in the Document

1. Follow these steps to scroll in the document:

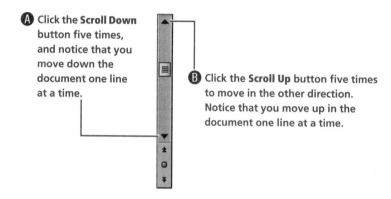

Ⓐ Click the **Scroll Down** button five times, and notice that you move down the document one line at a time.

Ⓑ Click the **Scroll Up** button five times to move in the other direction. Notice that you move up in the document one line at a time.

2. Position the **I-beam** I mouse pointer in the body of the document.
   Notice that while the mouse pointer looks like an I-beam when it's inside the document, it looks like a white arrow when it is in the document's left margin. The pointer must have the I-beam shape before you can reposition the insertion point.

Position the Insertion Point

3. Click the **I-beam** I anywhere in the document to position the blinking insertion point.

4. Move the **mouse pointer** into the left margin area. The white ⬩ arrow shape is now visible.

5. Position the **I-beam** I in the first line of the body of the document, and click the **left** mouse button.
   The insertion point appears just where you clicked. If the background is highlighted, you accidentally selected the text. Deselect by clicking the mouse pointer in the document background.

6. Click the open part of the **scroll bar** below the scroll box to move down one screen, as shown in the illustration to the right.

Use the Scroll Box and the Next Page/Previous Page Buttons

7. Drag the **scroll box** to the bottom of the scroll bar with the mouse pointer.
   Notice that the insertion point is not blinking anywhere on the screen because all you have done is scroll through the document. You have not repositioned the insertion point yet.

8. Click any open part of the **scroll bar** above the scroll box, then click the **I-beam** I at the end of the text to position the insertion point on the last page.

9. Drag the **scroll box** to the top of the scroll bar, and click the **I-beam** I in front of the first word of the first paragraph.

10. Click the **Next Page** ⬇ button to move to the top of page 2.
The insertion point moves with you when you use the Next Page and Previous Page buttons.

11. Click the **Previous Page** ⬆ button to move to the top of page 1.

Navigating with the Keyboard

Video Lesson labyrinthelab.com/videos

Whether you use the mouse or the keyboard to navigate through a document is a matter of personal preference. Navigating with the keyboard always moves the insertion point, so it will be with you when you arrive at your destination.

The following Quick Reference table provides keystrokes for moving quickly through a document.

QUICK REFERENCE	NAVIGATING WITH THE KEYBOARD		
Press	**To Move**	**Press**	**To Move**
→	One character to the right	Page Down	Down one screen
←	One character to the left	Page Up	Up one screen
Ctrl+→	One word to the right	Ctrl+End	To the end of the document
Ctrl+←	One word to the left	Ctrl+Home	To the beginning of the document
↓	Down one line	End	To the end of the line
↑	Up one line	Home	To the beginning of the line

DEVELOP YOUR SKILLS 1.5.2
Use the Keyboard to Navigate

In this exercise, you will use the keyboard to practice moving through a document.

Use the Arrow Keys

1. Click the **I-beam** I in the middle of the first line of the first paragraph.

2. Tap the **right arrow** → and **left arrow** ← keys three times to move to the right and left, one character at a time.

3. Tap the **down arrow** ↓ and **up arrow** ↑ keys three times to move down and then up, one row at a time.

Use Additional Keys

4. **Hold down** the Ctrl key and keep it down, then **tap** the Home key to move the insertion point to the beginning of the document. **Release** the Ctrl key.

5. Use the **arrow keys** to position the insertion point in the middle of the first line of the first paragraph.

6. **Hold down** the ⌈Ctrl⌉ key and keep it down, then tap the **left arrow** ⌈←⌉ key three times to move to the left, one word at a time. **Release** the ⌈Ctrl⌉ key.

7. **Hold down** the ⌈Ctrl⌉ key and keep it down, then tap the **right arrow** ⌈→⌉ key three times to move to the right, one word at a time. **Release** the ⌈Ctrl⌉ key.

8. **Tap** the ⌈Home⌉ key to move to the beginning of the line.

9. **Tap** the ⌈End⌉ key to move to the end of the line.

10. Spend a few moments **navigating** with the keyboard. Refer to the preceding Quick Reference table for some additional keystrokes.

11. **Hold down** the ⌈Ctrl⌉ key then **tap** the ⌈End⌉ key to move the insertion point to the end of the document. **Release** the ⌈Ctrl⌉ key.

12. Move the **insertion point** back to the beginning of the document.

1.6 Closing Documents

Video Lesson labyrinthelab.com/videos

You close a file by clicking the File tab and choosing the Close command from the menu. If you haven't saved your document, Word will prompt you to do so.

DEVELOP YOUR SKILLS 1.6.1
Close the Document

In this exercise, you will close a file.

1. **Click** the File tab, and then choose **Close** from the menu.

2. If Word asks you if you want to save the changes, click **Don't Save**.

3. If a blank document is open on the screen, use the same technique to **close** it.
   The document window always has this appearance when all documents are closed.

1.7 Starting a New, Blank Document

Video Lesson labyrinthelab.com/videos

You can click the **File** tab, and then choose the New command from the menu to open a new, blank document.

FROM THE KEYBOARD
Ctrl+N to start a new document

DEVELOP YOUR SKILLS 1.7.1
Start a New Document

In this exercise, you will open a new, blank document. There should not be any documents in the Word window at this time.

1. **Click** the **File** tab, and then choose **New** from the menu.

2. When the New Document dialog box appears, **double-click** the Blank Document icon to display the new document.
   Now you will close the new document and try using the shortcut keystrokes to start another new document.

3. **Click** the **File** tab, and then choose **Close** from the menu.

4. **Hold down** the Ctrl key and **tap** the N on your keyboard to open a new document.

5. Leave this document **open**.

1.8 Getting Help in Word 2010

Video Lesson labyrinthelab.com/videos

The Microsoft Word Help button appears in the upper-right corner of the Word screen. Clicking the Help button opens the Word Help window where you can browse through a Table of Contents, click links to access a variety of topics, or type a term in the search box and let the system find the answer for you.

Use Word Help

In this exercise you will practice working with several Help techniques.

1. Click the **Help** ⓦ button in the upper-right corner of the Word window.

2. Follow these steps for an overview of Word Help:

Ⓐ Some of these toolbar buttons are like ones you may already be familiar with from using a web browser. Click the **mouse pointer** on the top frame of the Word Help window to activate it, and then **hover** the mouse pointer over buttons to see **ToolTips** describing their purpose. The Table of Contents is not visible the first time you use Help; however, you can use the Table of Contents button to display it.

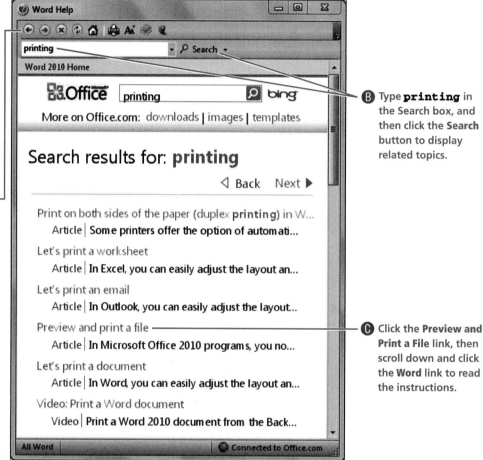

Ⓑ Type **printing** in the Search box, and then click the **Search** button to display related topics.

Ⓒ Click the **Preview and Print a File** link, then scroll down and click the **Word** link to read the instructions.

3. Click the **Close** ❎ button in the upper-right corner of the Word Help window.

1.9 Exiting from Word

Video Lesson   labyrinthelab.com/videos

Clicking the [File] tab and then clicking the [X Exit] button closes the Word application. It's important to exit Word in an orderly fashion. Turning off your computer before exiting Word could cause you to lose data.

You can also use the Close button in the upper-right corner of the window to close Word.

DEVELOP YOUR SKILLS 1.9.1
Exit from Word

In this exercise, you will exit from Word. Since the blank document on the screen has not been modified, you won't bother saving it.

1. **Click** the [File] tab.

2. **Click** the [X Exit] button at the bottom of the list.

3. When Word prompts you to save changes, click **Don't Save**.
   Word closes and the Windows Desktop appears.

1.10 Concepts Review

Concepts Review   labyrinthelab.com/word10

To check your knowledge of the key concepts introduced in this lesson, complete the Concepts Review quiz by going to the URL listed above. If your classroom is using Labyrinth eLab, you may complete the Concepts Review quiz from within your eLab course.

Reinforce Your Skills

REINFORCE YOUR SKILLS 1.1

Identify Elements of the Word 2010 Window

In this exercise, you will practice using correct terminology with parts of the Word screen. It's important to use the right terms when talking about the Word application. If, for example, you need to discuss an issue with people in your IT department, they can help you faster if they are clear on what you are talking about.

1. Start **Word 2010**.

2. Using the table to the right of the illustration, write down the correct terms for items **A through E**.

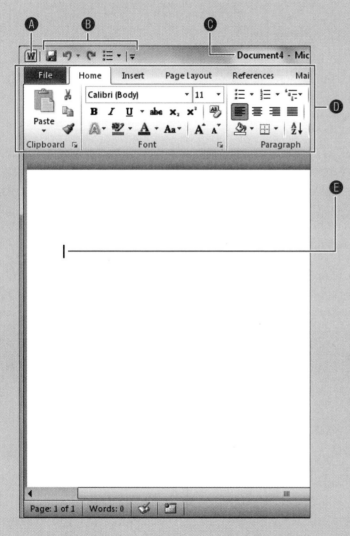

Letter	Term
A	
B	
C	
D	
E	

Use Word Help

In this exercise, you will work with the Word Help window to find information that can assist you as you work.

1. Click the **Microsoft Word Help** 📖 button in the upper-right corner of the Word window.

Use the Browse Word Help Window

Now you'll review opening a file in another file format. Your links may be in different locations depending on if your computer is online or not.

2. Click the **File Migration** link; then scroll down and click the **Use Word to Open or Save a File in Another File Format** link and read the topic.

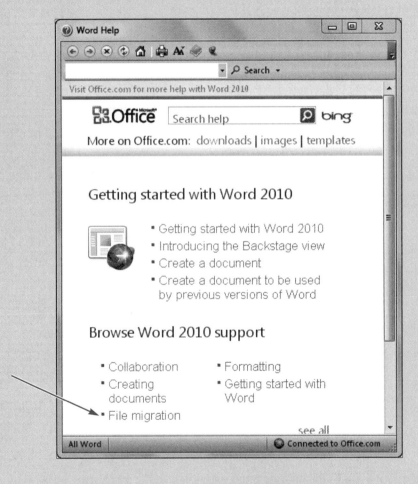

3. Scroll up and click the **Word 2010 Home** link at the top of the pane to return to the Browse Word Help pane.

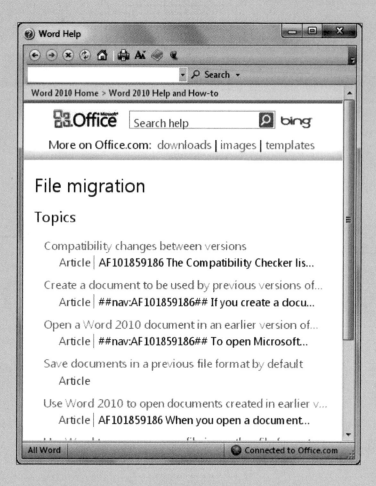

4. Click the **Creating Documents** link in the Word Help window.

5. Click the **Create a Document** link.

6. **Scroll down** to see the major topics that are covered.

Search for Help

7. Follow these steps to locate the Set the Default Font topic:

Ⓐ Click the **I-beam** in this box, located in the upper-left corner of the Word Help window, and type **default font**.

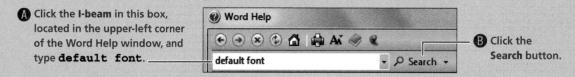

Ⓑ Click the **Search** button.

8. Click the **Set the Default Font** link in the Word Help window to view the topic.

9. **Scroll down** and take a moment to read the first few entries.

10. Click the **Close** X button in the upper-right corner of the Word Help window.

Navigate in a Document

In this exercise, you will use a letter that an exchange student in Paris wrote to his friend. It's a long letter, so it will provide good practice for navigating.

1. **Click** the [File] tab and choose **Open** from the menu.

2. When the Open dialog box appears, if necessary, **navigate** to your file storage location and **open** the Lesson 01 folder.

3. **Double-click** to open the file named rs-Exchange Student.

Navigate with the Scroll Bar

4. Click the **Next Page** [⯯] button at the bottom of the scroll bar to move to the top of page 2.

5. Click the **scroll bar** below the scroll box to move down one screen.

6. Drag the **scroll box** to the top of the scroll bar, and **click** for an insertion point at the beginning of the document.

7. Click the **Scroll Down** [▼] button, and hold the mouse button down to scroll quickly through the document.

8. Click the **Previous Page** [⯅] button enough times to return to the top of the document.

Navigate with the Keyboard

9. Tap the **down arrow** [↓] key twice to move to the beginning of the first paragraph.

10. **Tap** the [End] key to move the insertion point to the end of the line.

11. **Tap** the [Home] key to move to the beginning of the line.

12. **Tap** [Ctrl]+[End] to place the insertion point at the end of the document.

13. **Tap** [Ctrl]+[Home] to move to the top of the document.

14. If you press and hold the arrow keys, the insertion point moves quickly through the document. **Press and hold** the [↓] key long enough to move to the beginning of the second paragraph.

15. **Hold down** the [Ctrl] key and **tap** the [→] key three times to move to the right, one word at a time.

16. Please leave this document **open** for the next exercise.

Work with the Quick Access Toolbar

In this exercise, you will move the Quick Access toolbar below the Ribbon, and you will customize the toolbar by adding a button to it.

Before You Begin: The rs-Exchange Student document should be open in Word.

1. Follow these steps to move the Quick Access toolbar:

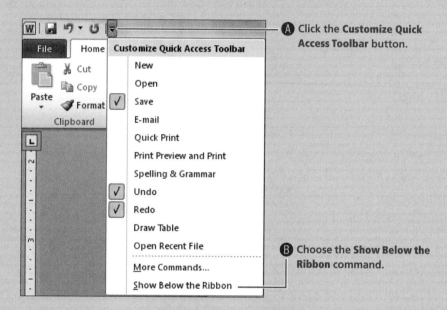

Ⓐ Click the **Customize Quick Access Toolbar** button.

Ⓑ Choose the **Show Below the Ribbon** command.

Now you will return the toolbar to its original position.

2. Click the **drop-down arrow** at the right edge of the toolbar, and choose **Show Above the Ribbon** from the menu.
   Next you'll add a button to the Quick Access toolbar.

3. Make sure you're on the **Home** tab. If not, **click** the tab to bring it to the foreground.

4. Follow these steps to add the **Clear Formatting** button to the toolbar:

Ⓐ **Right-click** the Clear Formatting button in the Font group.

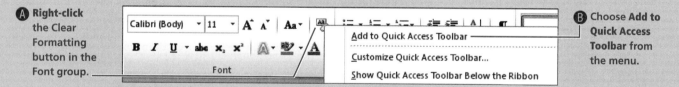

Ⓑ Choose **Add to Quick Access Toolbar** from the menu.

The button now appears on the toolbar.

5. Ask your instructor to inspect your work and initial here to verify the placement of the Clear Formatting button on the toolbar. _____
   Next you will remove the button you just added to the toolbar.

6. Place the mouse pointer over the **Clear Formatting** button on the Quick Access toolbar and click the **right** mouse button.

7. Choose **Remove from Quick Access Toolbar** from the menu.

8. Please leave this document **open** for the next exercise.

Apply Your Skills

Use Help to Learn About Print Preview

In this exercise, you will explore Help to learn how to preview a document before printing it.

Before You Begin: The rs-Exchange Student document should be open in Word.

1. Use Help's **Search** feature to locate information about Print Preview.

2. Open the **Print Preview** window by following the instructions in the Help window.

3. Practice using the commands in the **Zoom** group on the Ribbon to view your document in various magnifications.

4. Zoom your document to **250%**, and then ask your instructor to verify the zoom magnification and initial this step. _____

5. **Close** Print Preview, and leave this document **open** for the next exercise.

6. **Close** the Help window.

Ribbon Terminology

In this exercise, you will review terminology relating to the Ribbon. Feel free to refer back in this lesson or to use Word's Help feature to find the correct terms.

1. List the names of the tabs on the Ribbon.

   _____

   _____

   _____

   _____

   _____

   _____

   _____

2. List three commands in the Paragraph group of the Home tab.

   _____

   _____

   _____

3. Define contextual tabs.

   _____

   _____

4. Ask your instructor to verify your answers and initial this exercise. _____

5. Leave the rs-Exchange Student document open for the next exercise.

Customize the Ribbon

In this exercise, you will customize the Ribbon by adding a new tab and group.

1. Add a new **tab** named **Favorites** with a new **group** named **Formatting**.

2. Place the Favorites tab between the **Home** and **Insert** tabs on the Ribbon.

3. Place three **formatting commands** to the new Formatting group.

4. **Restore** all Ribbon defaults by removing any customizations.

5. **Close** the rs-Exchange Student document. If you are prompted to save, do not.

Critical Thinking & Work-Readiness Skills

In the course of working through the following Microsoft Office-based Critical Thinking exercises, you will also be utilizing various work-readiness skills, some of which are listed next to each exercise. Go to labyrinthelab.com/workreadiness *to learn more about the work-readiness skills.*

1.1 Use Help

WORK-READINESS SKILLS APPLIED

- Acquiring and evaluating information
- Thinking creatively
- Knowing how to learn

Elise Ferrer, one of My Virtual Campus' tech support specialists, has been asked to help with the company's migration from Office 2007 to Office 2010. She decides to provide a "cheat sheet" of online help tutorials to aid the employees using Word. Start Word, create a new, blank document, and use Word's Help feature to locate five basic topics for this purpose. Use a sheet of notebook paper and a pen to record the five links to the online help topics you found.

1.2 Customize the Ribbon

WORK-READINESS SKILLS APPLIED

- Solving problems
- Thinking creatively
- Showing responsibility

To help the employees in the marketing department work more efficiently, Elise customizes their Ribbons by adding a custom tab. Create a new tab in Word called **Marketing** and position it before the Home tab. Create a group in the custom tab named **Marketing Tasks**. Add five commands to the Marketing Tasks group that you think might be useful for someone working in a marketing department (they will be opening, editing, and formatting documents, in addition to inserting pictures). On a sheet of notebook paper, write down the five commands you selected and explain why you think those particular commands would be helpful for someone in the marketing department. Reset the Ribbon to its default setting when you are finished.

1.3 Customize the Interface

WORK-READINESS SKILLS APPLIED

- Managing the self
- Showing responsibility
- Participating as a member of a team

Elise decides to customize the Word interface of her own computer to help her work more efficiently. Practice minimizing and maximizing the Ribbon. Display the Quick Access toolbar both above and below the Ribbon. Add or remove buttons from the Quick Access toolbar. On a sheet of notebook paper, draw a simple sketch of your preferred settings for the Ribbon and Quick Access toolbar. If applicable, exchange papers with a partner and configure your Word interface according to your partner's sketch. Reset the Ribbon and Quick Access toolbar to their default states when you are finished.

Creating and Editing Business Letters

LEARNING OBJECTIVES

After studying this lesson, you will be able to:

- Type a professional business letter
- Save a document
- Select and edit text
- Use the AutoCorrect feature
- Set AutoFormat as You Type options
- Copy and move text
- Set Page Layout options
- Preview a document

In this lesson, you will create business letters while learning proper business document formatting. You will also learn fundamental techniques of entering and editing text, copying and moving text, and saving and printing documents. In addition, you will learn to use Word's AutoCorrect tool to insert frequently used text and control automatic formatting that is applied as you type.

Taking Care with Business Letters

Rob Maloney just landed his job as a customer service representative in the Sales Department at My Virtual Campus. He is working for the sales manager, Bruce Carter. A new prospect, Richmond University, has expressed interest in the networking website that My Virtual Campus sells. Mr. Carter has asked Rob to prepare a standard letter for potential new clients, thanking them for their interest and providing information about the website.

Rob starts by referring to his business writing class textbook to ensure that he formats the letter correctly for a good first impression and a professional appearance.

November 24, 2012

Ms. Paige Daniels
Richmond University
15751 Meadow Lane
Chester Allen, VA 23333

Dear Ms. Daniels:

Travis Mayfield referred you to us after he spoke to you about our extraordinary product. I want to take this opportunity to personally thank you for considering My Virtual Campus' social-networking website for your institution. As Travis may have mentioned, we pride ourselves in providing the latest in technology as well as excellent customer service with satisfaction guaranteed.

Enclosed you will find information to review regarding the features of the website. After reading the material, please contact our sales manager, Bruce Carter, at your earliest convenience to discuss your options. Thank you again for considering our amazing website.

Sincerely,

Rob Maloney
Customer Service Representative
Sales Department

rm
Enclosures (2)
cc: Bruce Carter

2.1 Defining Typical Business Letter Styles

Video Lesson labyrinthelab.com/videos

There are several acceptable styles of business letters. The styles discussed in this text include block, modified block standard format, and modified block indented paragraphs. All business letters contain the same or similar elements, but with varied formatting. The following styles are described in this section:

- Block Style
- Modified Block Style—Standard Format
- Modified Block Style—Indented Paragraphs

Block Style

The following illustration outlines the parts of the block style business letter.

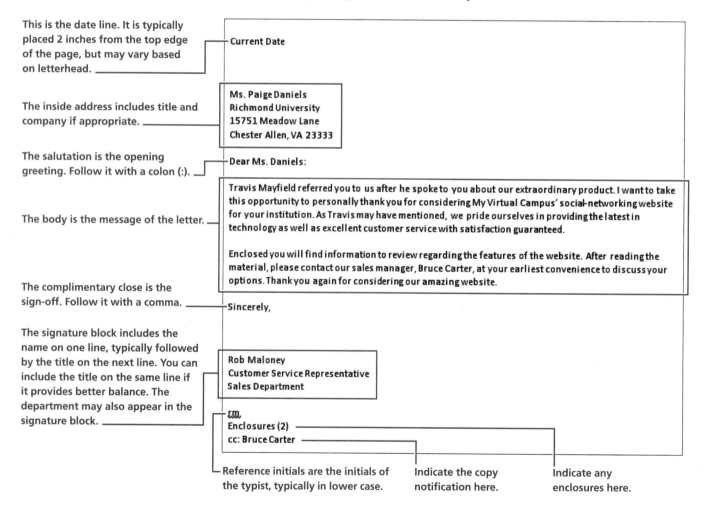

This is the date line. It is typically placed 2 inches from the top edge of the page, but may vary based on letterhead.

Current Date

The inside address includes title and company if appropriate.

Ms. Paige Daniels
Richmond University
15751 Meadow Lane
Chester Allen, VA 23333

The salutation is the opening greeting. Follow it with a colon (:).

Dear Ms. Daniels:

The body is the message of the letter.

Travis Mayfield referred you to us after he spoke to you about our extraordinary product. I want to take this opportunity to personally thank you for considering My Virtual Campus' social-networking website for your institution. As Travis may have mentioned, we pride ourselves in providing the latest in technology as well as excellent customer service with satisfaction guaranteed.

Enclosed you will find information to review regarding the features of the website. After reading the material, please contact our sales manager, Bruce Carter, at your earliest convenience to discuss your options. Thank you again for considering our amazing website.

The complimentary close is the sign-off. Follow it with a comma.

Sincerely,

The signature block includes the name on one line, typically followed by the title on the next line. You can include the title on the same line if it provides better balance. The department may also appear in the signature block.

Rob Maloney
Customer Service Representative
Sales Department

rm
Enclosures (2)
cc: Bruce Carter

Reference initials are the initials of the typist, typically in lower case.

Indicate the copy notification here.

Indicate any enclosures here.

Modified Block Style—Standard Format

The following illustration outlines the differences in the standard modified block style business letter from the block style business letter.

The date line, the complimentary close, and the signature block begin at the 3 ½ inch mark on the ruler. All other lines begin at the left margin.

November 24, 2012

Ms. Paige Daniels
Richmond University
15751 Meadow Lane
Chester Allen, VA 23333

Dear Ms. Daniels:

Travis Mayfield referred you to us after he spoke to you about our extraordinary product. I want to take this opportunity to personally thank you for considering My Virtual Campus' social-networking website for your institution. As Travis may have mentioned, we pride ourselves in providing the latest in technology as well as excellent customer service with satisfaction guaranteed.

Enclosed you will find information to review regarding the features of the website. After reading the material, please contact our sales manager, Bruce Carter, at your earliest convenience to discuss your options. Thank you again for considering our amazing website.

Sincerely,

Rob Maloney
Customer Service Representative
Sales Department

rm
Enclosures (2)
cc: Bruce Carter

Modified Block Style—Indented Paragraphs

The following illustration shows the modified block style business letter with indented paragraphs.

November 24, 2012

Ms. Paige Daniels
Richmond University
15751 Meadow Lane
Chester Allen, VA 23333

Dear Ms. Daniels:

In this format, the first lines of the body paragraphs are indented one-half inch.

    Travis Mayfield referred you to us after he spoke to you about our extraordinary product. I want to take this opportunity to personally thank you for considering My Virtual Campus' social-networking website for your institution. As Travis may have mentioned, we pride ourselves in providing the latest in technology as well as excellent customer service with satisfaction guaranteed.

    Enclosed you will find information to review regarding the features of the website. After reading the material, please contact our sales manager, Bruce Carter, at your earliest convenience to discuss your options. Thank you again for considering our amazing website.

Sincerely,

Rob Maloney
Customer Service Representative
Sales Department

rm
Enclosures (2)
cc: Bruce Carter

2.2 Inserting Text

Video Lesson labyrinthelab.com/videos

You always insert text into a Word document at the flashing insertion point. Therefore, you must position the insertion point at the desired location before typing.

AutoComplete

Word's AutoComplete feature does some of your typing for you. It recognizes certain words and phrases, such as names of months and names of days, and offers to complete them for you, as shown here.

As you begin typing the month November, AutoComplete offers to finish typing it out.

 AutoComplete does not offer to complete the months March through July.

You accept AutoComplete suggestions by tapping Enter. If you choose to ignore the suggestion, just keep typing, and the suggestion will disappear.

Using the Enter Key

You use Enter to begin a new paragraph or to insert blank lines in a document. Word considers anything that ends by tapping Enter to be a paragraph. Thus, short lines such as a date line, an inside address, or even blank lines themselves are considered paragraphs.

Tapping Enter inserts a paragraph ¶ symbol in a document. These symbols are visible when you display formatting marks.

Showing Formatting Marks

The Show/Hide ¶ button in the Paragraph group of the Home tab shows or hides formatting marks. Although they appear on the screen, you will not see them in the printed document. Marks include dots representing spaces between words, paragraph symbols that appear when you tap Enter, and arrows that represent tabs.

Viewing these characters can be important when editing a document. You may need to see the nonprinting characters to determine whether the space between two words was created with the Spacebar or Tab. The following illustrations show the location of the Show/Hide button and the characters that appear when you tap the Spacebar, the Enter key, or the Tab key.

Show/Hide button

These symbols are paragraph marks. They appear whenever you tap Enter.

The dots between words are inserted when you tap the Spacebar.

Tabs are represented by small arrows.

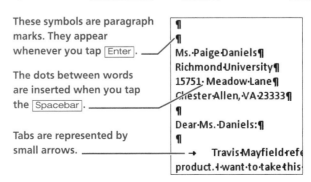

Spacing in Letters

In Word 2007, new default line spacing was introduced. This change adjusted the default line spacing to 1.15 rather than the standard single spacing and added an extra 10 points (a little more than an eighth of an inch) at the end of paragraphs. Therefore, rather that tapping [Enter] twice at the end of a paragraph, you just tap [Enter] once, and Word adds the extra spacing.

Apply Traditional Spacing Using the Line Spacing Button

When writing letters, a traditional, more compact look (without the additional spacing) is still considered appropriate. Therefore, when you begin a letter, you may wish to switch to single (1.0) spacing and remove the extra space after paragraphs by choosing the options shown in the following figure.

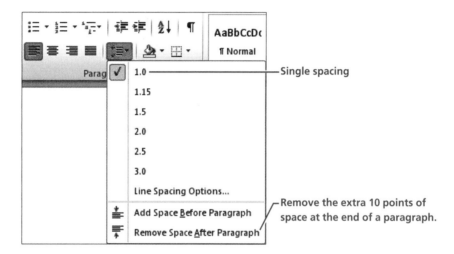

Apply these settings when you wish to type a more compact, traditional letter.

Apply Traditional Spacing Using the No Spacing Style

An alternative to using the Line Spacing button to achieve traditional spacing is to apply the No Spacing style located in the Styles group of the Home tab on the Ribbon, as shown here.

When you begin a new document, click the No Spacing icon on the Ribbon to achieve traditional spacing.

The exercises in this lesson use the Line Spacing button to set traditional spacing; however, feel free to use this alternate method instead if you prefer.

Word Wrap

If you continue typing after the insertion point reaches the end of a line, Word automatically wraps the insertion point to the beginning of the next line. If you let Word Wrap format your paragraph initially, the paragraph will also reformat correctly as you insert or delete text.

Creating an Envelope

Microsoft Word is very smart and versatile when it comes to creating envelopes. For example, when you type a business letter with the recipient's name and address at the top of it, Word recognizes this as the delivery address. Word also gives you two options: print the address directly onto the envelope or insert the envelope at the top of the document in a separate section. The latter option means you can open the letter at any time and the envelope is there, ready for you to print it.

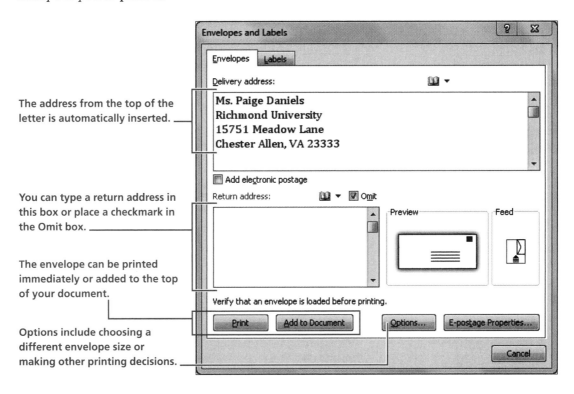

The address from the top of the letter is automatically inserted.

You can type a return address in this box or place a checkmark in the Omit box.

The envelope can be printed immediately or added to the top of your document.

Options include choosing a different envelope size or making other printing decisions.

Return Address

The Envelopes and Labels dialog box allows you to type a return address and keep it as the default. If you don't want the default return address to print on the envelope, you must ensure the Omit checkbox is unchecked in the dialog box.

If a default return address has not been established or the Return Address box is empty, clicking the Omit checkbox is not necessary. By default, the Omit checkbox is already checked.

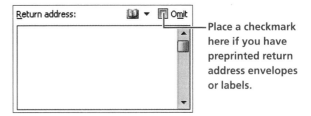

Place a checkmark here if you have preprinted return address envelopes or labels.

When you enter a return address, you will be prompted to save it as the default so you don't have to type it each time you create an envelope.

Type a Letter and an Envelope

In this exercise, you will display formatting marks, adjust spacing, use AutoComplete, work with the Enter *key, and let Word Wrap do its job. Finally, you will create an envelope for the letter.*

Display Nonprinting Characters and Modify Line Spacing

1. Start **Word**. Make sure the Word window is **maximized** ▣.

2. Choose **Home→Paragraph→Show/Hide** ¶ from the Ribbon, as shown to the right.

   New documents contain a paragraph symbol; you won't see it if you don't turn on the Show/Hide feature. Paragraph symbols carry formatting in them. For a new document, formatting includes default spacing of 1.15 lines and extra space at the end of a paragraph.

   In the next step, you'll select (highlight) the paragraph symbol and reformat it, changing the default line spacing to 1.0 and removing additional space after a paragraph.

3. Position the **I-beam** Ⅰ left of the paragraph symbol, **press and hold** the mouse button, **drag** to the right to select (highlight) the paragraph symbol, and then **release** the mouse button.

4. Follow these steps to reformat the paragraph symbol:

   Ⓐ Choose **Home→ Paragraph→Line and Paragraph Spacing menu ▼** (not the main part of the button) from the Ribbon.

   Ⓑ Choose the **1.0** option.

   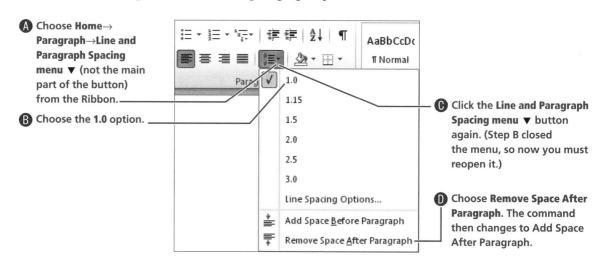

   Ⓒ Click the **Line and Paragraph Spacing menu ▼** button again. (Step B closed the menu, so now you must reopen it.)

   Ⓓ Choose **Remove Space After Paragraph**. The command then changes to Add Space After Paragraph.

Turn On the Ruler and Type the Letter

5. Click the **View Ruler** 🔲 button at the top of the vertical scroll bar to display the ruler.

6. **Tap** Enter five times to place the insertion point 2 inches from the top of the page (at approximately the 1 inch mark on the vertical ruler).

7. Start typing **Nove**, but stop when AutoComplete displays a pop-up tip.
   AutoComplete suggests the word it thinks you are typing and offers to complete it.

8. **Tap** Enter to automatically insert November into the letter.

9. Finish **typing** the date as **November 24, 2012**.

10. Continue **typing** the letter as shown in the following illustration, **tapping** Enter wherever you see a paragraph symbol.

If you catch a typo, you can tap the Backspace *key enough times to remove the error, and then continue typing.*

```
¶
¶
¶
¶
¶
November·24,·2012¶
¶
¶
¶
Ms.·Paige·Daniels¶
Richmond·University¶
15751·Meadow·Lane¶
Chester·Allen,·VA·23333¶
¶
Dear·Ms.·Daniels:¶
¶
```

11. **Type** the first body paragraph in the following illustration. Let Word Wrap do its thing, and then **tap** Enter twice at the end of the paragraph.

```
Travis·Mayfield·referred·you·to·us·after·he·spoke·to·you·yesterday·about·our·extraordinary·product.·I·
want·to·take·this·opportunity·to·thank·you·for·considering·My·Virtual·Campus'·social·networking·
website·for·your·institution.·As·Travis·may·have·mentioned,·we·pride·ourselves·in·providing·the·latest·in·
technology·as·well·as·excellent·customer·service.¶
¶
```

 If you see a wavy red line, that is Word's way of telling you that a word *might* be misspelled. If a term is not in Word's dictionary, it is marked as a possible error, even if it is spelled correctly. Wavy green lines indicate possible grammatical errors. Ignore red and green wavy lines for now.

12. Continue **typing** the letter, **tapping** Enter where you see a paragraph symbol.

```
I·have·enclosed·information·for·your·review·regarding·the·various·features·of·the·website.·After·reading·
the·material,·please·contact·our·sales·manager,·ASAP,·to·discuss·your·options.·Thank·you·again·for·
considering·our·amazing·website.¶
¶
Yours·truly,¶
¶
¶
¶
Rob·Maloney¶
Customer·Service·Representative¶
Sales·Department¶
```

Create the Envelope

Now you will create an envelope for the letter and add it to the top of the document.

13. **Tap** `Ctrl`+`Home` to place the insertion point at the top of the document, then choose **Mailings→Create→Envelopes** from the Ribbon.

14. Follow these steps to add an envelope to the document with no return address:

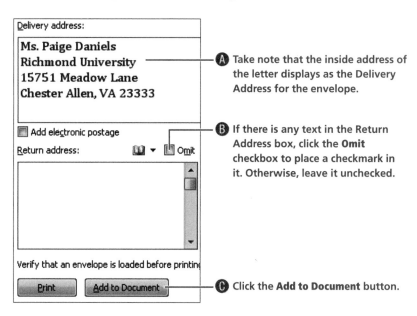

Delivery address:

Ms. Paige Daniels
Richmond University
15751 Meadow Lane
Chester Allen, VA 23333

A Take note that the inside address of the letter displays as the Delivery Address for the envelope.

☐ Add electronic postage

Return address: ▼   Omit

B If there is any text in the Return Address box, click the **Omit** checkbox to place a checkmark in it. Otherwise, leave it unchecked.

Verify that an envelope is loaded before printing

Print   Add to Document

C Click the **Add to Document** button.

Notice that the envelope has been added to the top of the document. When you save the document, the envelope is saved with it so you may print it at any time.

15. Click the **Undo** button to remove the envelope from the document.

16. Choose **Home→Paragraph→Show/Hide** ¶ to turn off the formatting marks.

Feel free to turn the Show/Hide feature on or off as you see fit throughout this course.

2.3 Saving Your Work

Video Lesson labyrinthelab.com/videos

It's important to save your documents frequently! Power outages and accidents can result in lost data. Documents are saved to storage locations such as hard drives and USB flash drives.

The Save Command

There are three primary commands used to save Word documents:

- The Save 🖫 button on the Quick Access toolbar
- The File→Save command
- The File→Save As command

When you save a document for the first time, the Save As dialog box appears. The following illustration describes significant features of the new Save As dialog box.

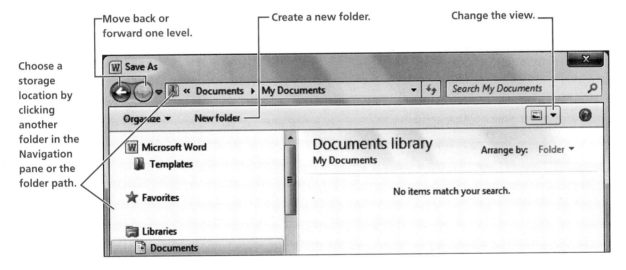

Move back or forward one level. Create a new folder. Change the view.

Choose a storage location by clicking another folder in the Navigation pane or the folder path.

Save Compared to Save As

While the Save and Save As commands are quite similar, each has a specific use. If the document was never saved, Word displays the Save As dialog box, where you specify the name and storage location of the document. If the document was previously saved, choosing the Save command again replaces the prior version with the edited one, without displaying the Save As dialog box. You can also use Save As to save a copy of a document, giving it a new file-name and/or a new storage location.

Word's DOCX File Format

A file format is a technique for saving computer data. Word 2003 and earlier versions saved documents in the *doc* format. Word 2007 introduced a new file format: *docx*. This is important because users of Word 2003 and prior versions may not be able to read Word files in the *docx* format. However, you can choose to save your document in the older *doc* file format, thus enabling someone with an older version of Word to open the file without installing special software. Also, when you open a document created in Word 2007, the title bar displays

Compatibility Mode next to the actual title. This means certain Word 2010 features not compatible with 2007 are turned off while working in the document.

Word 2003 users can download a compatibility pack from the Microsoft website that allows them to open, edit, save, and create files in the docx file format.

DEVELOP YOUR SKILLS 2.3.1

Save the Letter

In this exercise, you will save the letter you created in the previous exercise.

1. Click the **Save** 💾 button on the Quick Access toolbar.
   Word displays the Save As dialog box, since this is the first time you are saving this document. Once the file is named, this button will simply save the current version of the file over the old version.

2. Follow these steps to save the letter:
   Keep in mind that your dialog box may contain more files than shown here.

Ⓐ Click in the **Navigation pane,** and open the Lesson 02 folder on your file storage location.

Ⓑ Word always proposes the first line of text as the filename. Type the name **Daniels Letter** and it will replace the proposed name. (If you switched file storage locations, you may need to click in the **File Name** box, **delete** the proposed name with the ⌦ Delete or ⌫ Backspace key, and then **type** the new name.)

Ⓒ Click the **Save** button.

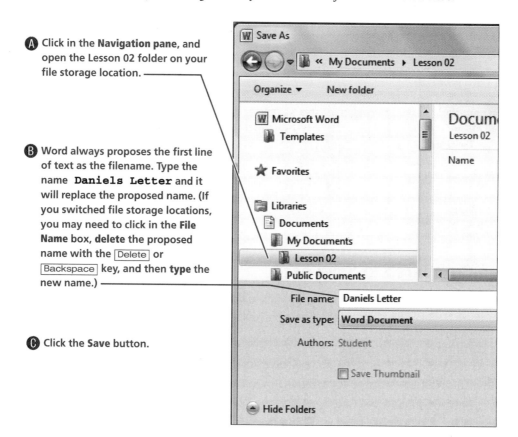

3. Leave the file **open** for the next exercise.

2.4 Selecting Text

Video Lesson labyrinthelab.com/videos

You must select (highlight) text if you wish to perform some action on it. Suppose you want to delete an entire line. You would select the line first, and then tap Delete .

Selection Techniques

Word provides many selection techniques; some use the mouse, and some use the keyboard. Use the keyboard techniques if you have difficulty controlling the mouse. Deselect text by clicking in the text area of the document or by tapping an arrow key. The following Quick Reference table illustrates various selection techniques.

QUICK REFERENCE	WORKING WITH SELECTION TECHNIQUES
Item to Be Selected	**Mouse Technique**
One word	Double-click the word.
Continuous block of text	Press and hold the left mouse button while dragging the I-beam over the desired text.
A line	Place the mouse pointer in the margin to the left of the line. Click when the pointer is shaped like an arrow.
A sentence	Hold down Ctrl and click the mouse pointer anywhere in the sentence.
One paragraph	Position the mouse pointer in the margin to the left of the paragraph and double-click, or triple-click anywhere in the paragraph.
Multiple paragraphs	Position the mouse pointer in the left margin and drag up or down when the pointer is shaped like an arrow, or drag the I-beam over the desired paragraphs.
Entire document	Triple-click in the left margin, or make sure no text is selected and then press and hold Ctrl and click in the left margin.
Nonadjacent areas	Select the first block of text, and then press and hold Ctrl while dragging over additional blocks of text.
Item to Be Selected	**Keyboard Technique**
One word	Click at the beginning of the word, and then press and hold Shift + Ctrl while tapping →.
Continuous block of text	Click at the beginning of the text, and then press and hold Shift while tapping any arrow key. You can also click at the beginning of the text, press and hold Shift, and click at the end of the selection.
A line	Press Shift + End to select from the insertion point to the end of the line. Press Shift + Home to select from the insertion point to the beginning of the line.
Entire document	Press Ctrl + A to execute the Select All command, or press Ctrl and click in the left margin.

Select Text

In this exercise, you will practice various selection techniques using the letter you just created. Selecting text causes the Mini toolbar to fade in. You can ignore it for now.

Select Using the Left Margin

1. Follow these steps to select text using the left margin:

Ⓐ Point outside the margin of the first line of the inside address.

Ⓑ Click once to select the entire line.

Ms. Paige Daniels
Richmond University
15751 Meadow Lane
Chester Allen, VA 23333

Ⓒ Make sure the pointer tilts to the **right**, and then **click** once to select this line. (Notice that the previously selected line is no longer selected.)

Dear Ms. Daniels:

Travis Mayfield referred you to us after he spoke to you yesterday about our extraordinary product. I want to take this opportunity to thank you for considering My Virtual Campus' social-networking website for your institution. As Travis may have mentioned, we pride ourselves in providing the latest in technology as well as excellent customer service.

Ⓓ Select this paragraph by **double-clicking** in front of it, using the white selection arrow.

2. Making sure the mouse pointer tilts to the **right** 𝔑, **drag** down the left margin. Be sure to **press and hold** the left mouse button as you drag. Then, **click** in the body of the document to deselect the text.

3. Move the **mouse pointer** back to the margin so it is tilting to the **right** 𝔑, then **triple-click** anywhere in the left margin.
Word selects the entire document.

4. **Click** once anywhere in the body of the document to deselect it.

Select Words

5. Point on any word with the **I-beam** I, and then **double-click** to select it.

6. **Double-click** a different word, and notice that the previous word is deselected.

Nonadjacent Selections

You can also select multiple locations within a document.

7. **Double-click** to select one word.

8. With one word selected, **press and hold** the ⌈Ctrl⌉ key while you **double-click** to select another word, and then **release** the ⌈Ctrl⌉ key.
Both selections are active. You can select as many nonadjacent areas of a document as desired using this technique. This can be quite useful when formatting documents.

Drag to Select

9. Follow these steps to drag and select a block of text:

A Position the **I-beam** here, just in front of *Travis Mayfield*.... Make sure the I-beam is visible, not the right-tilting arrow.

B **Press and hold** down the mouse button, and then **drag to the right** until the phrase *Travis Mayfield referred you to us after he spoke to you* is selected.

I Travis Mayfield referred you to us after he spoke to you yesterday abo want to take this opportunity to thank you for considering My Virtual C website for your institution. As Travis may have mentioned, we pride o

C **Release** the mouse button; the text remains selected.

2.5 Editing Text

Video Lesson   labyrinthelab.com/videos

Word offers many tools for editing documents, allowing you to insert and delete text and undo and redo work.

Inserting and Deleting Text

When you insert text in Word, existing text moves to the right as you type. You must position the insertion point before you begin typing.

Use Backspace and Delete to remove text. The Backspace key deletes *characters* to the left of the insertion point. The Delete key removes characters to the *right* of the insertion point. You can also remove an entire block of text by selecting it, and then tapping Delete or Backspace.

Using Undo and Redo

Word's Undo button lets you reverse your last editing or formatting change(s). You can reverse simple actions such as accidental text deletions, or you can reverse more complex actions, such as margin changes.

FROM THE KEYBOARD
Ctrl+Z to undo the last action

The Redo button reverses Undo. Use Redo when you undo an action and then change your mind.

The Undo menu ▼ button (see figure at right) displays a list of recent changes. You can undo multiple actions by dragging the mouse pointer over the desired items in the list. However, you must undo changes in the order in which they appear on the list.

Insert and Delete Text and Use Undo and Redo

In this exercise, you will insert and delete text. You will delete characters using both the Backspace *and* Delete *keys, and you will select and delete blocks of text. You will also use the Undo and Redo buttons on the Quick Access toolbar.*

1. In the first line of the first paragraph, **double-click** the word *yesterday,* as shown to the right, and then **tap** Delete to remove the word.

    spoke to you yesterday about
    for considering My Virtual Car

2. Click with the **I-beam** (not the right-tilted arrow) at the beginning of the word *thank* in the second line of the first paragraph of the first paragraph, type **personally**, and then **tap** the Spacebar.

3. Position the **insertion point** at the end of the first paragraph between the word *service* and the period at the end of the sentence.

4. **Tap** the Spacebar, and type **with satisfaction guaranteed**.

5. **Drag** to select the first three words of the second paragraph and then type **Enclosed you will find** to replace the selected text.

6. In the same line, position the **insertion point** after the word *your* and **tap** Backspace until the words *for your* are deleted, then type **to**.

7. **Double-click** the word *various* in the same line and **tap** Delete to remove it.

8. In the next line, **double-click** *ASAP,* and type **Bruce Carter, at your earliest convenience,** in its place.

9. Move the **mouse pointer** into the margin to the left of *Yours truly.*
    Remember, the mouse pointer is a white, right-tilted arrow when it's in the left margin.

10. **Click** once to select the line, and then type **Sincerely,** in its place.

Use Undo and Redo

11. You've decided that you prefer *Yours truly,* so click the **Undo** button on the Quick Access toolbar until you return to *Yours truly.*

12. Well, maybe *Sincerely* is better after all. Click the **Redo** button on the Quick Access toolbar until you return to *Sincerely.*

Save Your Changes

13. Click the **Save** button on the Quick Access toolbar to save your changes.

14. Leave the document **open** for the next exercise.

2.6 Working with AutoCorrect

Video Lesson labyrinthelab.com/videos

AutoCorrect is predefined text used for automatically correcting common spelling and capitalization errors. You may have noticed AutoCorrect changing the spelling of certain words while working through the last exercise.

The AutoCorrect feature corrects more than spelling errors. For example, you can set up an AutoCorrect entry to insert the phrase *as soon as possible* whenever you type *asap* and tap the Spacebar or certain other characters such as a Tab, Comma, or Period. AutoCorrect will also capitalize a word it thinks is the beginning of a sentence.

DEVELOP YOUR SKILLS 2.6.1
Use AutoCorrect

In this exercise, you will type some terms that AutoCorrect will fix for you.

1. **Tap** Ctrl + End to move the insertion point to the end of the document.

2. If necessary, **tap** Enter a few times to provide some space to practice.

3. **Type** the word **teh** and **tap** the Tab key.
   AutoCorrect corrects the mistake and capitalizes the word because it thinks it is the first word of a sentence.

4. **Type** the word **adn** and **tap** the Spacebar.

5. Now **select** and Delete the words you were just practicing with.

AutoCorrect Options Smart Tag

Video Lesson labyrinthelab.com/videos

Word uses smart tags, small buttons that pop up automatically, to provide menus of options that are in context with what you are doing at the time. One of those smart tags is the AutoCorrect Options smart tag.

If Word automatically corrects something that you don't want corrected, a smart tag option allows you to undo the change. For example, when Word automatically capitalizes the first C in the cc: line, you can quickly undo the capitalization, as shown here.

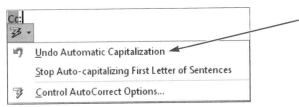

 You will see many smart tags as you work. If you do not want to use a smart tag, you can ignore it and it will disappear on its own.

Use the AutoCorrect Smart Tag

In this exercise, you will use the AutoCorrect Options smart tags.

1. Choose **Home→Paragraph→Show/Hide** ¶ to display formatting marks.
   The reference initials should appear on the second blank line following the signature block. Make sure two paragraph symbols appear, as shown here.

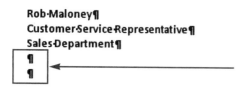

2. If necessary, position the **insertion point** and use Enter to create the blank line(s).

3. Position the **insertion point** next to the second paragraph symbol, and type **rm** as the reference initials, and then **tap** Enter.
   Notice what happened. Autocorrect capitalized the R, and it should not be capitalized.

4. Position the **mouse pointer** over the R, and you should see a small blue rectangle just below the R. Then **drag down** a little, and the AutoCorrect Options screen tip appears.

5. Click the **AutoCorrect Options** smart tag to display the menu shown below. (This is a delicate mouse move, so you may need to try it a couple of times.)

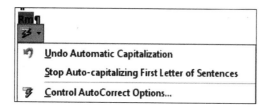

6. Choose **Undo Automatic Capitalization** from the menu.
   Notice that Word marks the initials with a wavy red line, indicating it's a possible spelling error. You can just ignore it.

7. Make sure the **insertion point** is on the blank line below the initials. Then **type** the enclosures notification, **Enclosures (2)**, and **tap** Enter.

8. **Save** 🖫 the document and leave it **open** for the next exercise.

Setting AutoCorrect Options

Video Lesson   labyrinthelab.com/videos

To display the AutoCorrect dialog box, choose the File tab to display the Backstage view and then click the Options tab at the bottom of the Navigation pane to open the Word Options window. The AutoCorrect Options button on the Proofing page opens the AutoCorrect dialog box.

Changing AutoCorrect Exceptions

There can be exceptions to the AutoCorrect options you set. For example, when the option Correct Two Initial Capitals is checked and you accidently type the first and second letter in capitals, AutoCorrect automatically corrects it for you. There are three types of exceptions you can set.

- **First Letter**—If you do not type the first letter of a new line as a capital, AutoCorrect fixes it for you automatically. However, you may at times need an exception to this rule. For example, at the bottom of a letter, after you type cc: to indicate a carbon copy, AutoCorrect automatically makes the first letter a capital.

- **Initial Caps**—The opposite of the First Letter option is when you type two capital letters and both should remain capitalized. AutoCorrect automatically corrects the second letter unless you add an exception. For example, when referring to user IDs, you would want the "D" to remain capitalized.

- **Other Corrections**—You can add words here that you do not want AutoCorrect to change, even if they are in the Replace as You Type List at the bottom of the AutoCorrect box. For example, your company may have a unique name or use special terminology.

When you create AutoCorrect entries in Word, the entries are also available for use in Microsoft Excel, PowerPoint, and Access.

In addition to correcting spelling errors, AutoCorrect makes these changes. Removing a checkmark from one of the checkboxes turns the feature off. ———————

This checkbox turns the AutoCorrect feature on or off. ———

Use the Replace and With boxes to create customized AutoText entries. ———

The AutoCorrect table contains AutoCorrect terms that are built into Word as well as your customized entries. ———

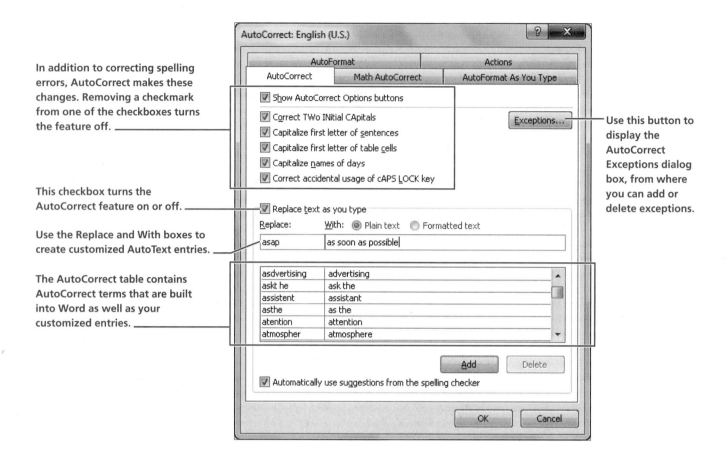

Use this button to display the AutoCorrect Exceptions dialog box, from where you can add or delete exceptions.

Customizing AutoCorrect

Word's AutoCorrect feature also lets you automatically insert customized text and special characters, and it is useful for replacing abbreviations with full phrases. For example, you could set up AutoCorrect to insert the name of your company whenever you type an abbreviation for it. You can also customize AutoCorrect by deleting entries that are installed with Word; however, please do not delete any in this classroom.

 Do not create an AutoCorrect entry with an abbreviation you may want to use on its own; for example, if you used *USA* as an abbreviation for *United States of America,* you could not use *USA* alone because every time you typed it, it would be replaced with *United States of America.*

DEVELOP YOUR SKILLS 2.6.3
Create a Custom AutoCorrect Entry

In this exercise, you will create a custom AutoCorrect entry. It's now time for the copy notification, and you plan to copy Bruce Carter. Since you work for him, you know you'll need to type his name frequently, so it's a perfect candidate for a custom AutoCorrect entry.

1. Click the **File** tab and then click Options at the bottom of the Navigation pane.

2. When the Word Options window opens, follow these steps to display the AutoCorrect dialog box:

Ⓐ Choose **Proofing** from the menu.   Ⓑ Click the **AutoCorrect Options** button.

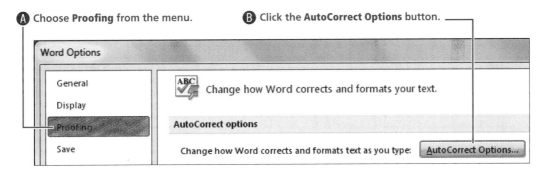

3. When the AutoCorrect dialog box appears, follow these steps to add a custom AutoCorrect entry:

Ⓐ Type **bmc** in the Replace box.

Ⓑ Type **Bruce Carter** in the With box.

Ⓒ Click the Add button.

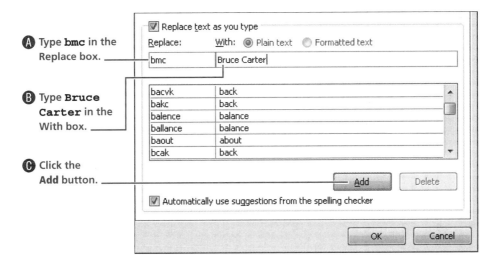

4. Click **OK** twice.

5. Type **cc:** and **tap** the Spacebar.

6. Use the **AutoCorrect Options** smart tag to undo the automatic capitalization.
Now you can try out the new AutoCorrect item you added in step 3.

7. Type **bmc** and **tap** Enter to automatically type the sales manager's name.

Delete the Custom AutoCorrect Entry

You can easily remove AutoCorrect entries, whether they are new custom entries you added or default entries you did not create originally.

8. Click the **File** tab and then click **Options** at the bottom of the Navigation pane.

9. Choose **Proofing** from the menu, and then click the **AutoCorrect Options** button in the right-hand pane.

10. Type **bmc** in the Replace box, which scrolls the list to Bruce Carter.

11. Click the **Delete** button in the bottom-right corner of the dialog box.

12. Click **OK** twice.

13. **Save** 🖫 the letter and leave it **open** for the next exercise.

Setting AutoFormat As You Type Options

Video Lesson labyrinthelab.com/videos

One of the tabs in the AutoCorrect dialog box is AutoFormat As You Type. You may have noticed certain formatting taking place automatically; this is happening because certain options are already set for you. For example, AutoFormat will replace a typed hyphen (-) with a dash (–), an ordinal (1st) with superscript (1st), or a fraction (1/2) with a fraction character (½). AutoFormat can also create an automatic bulleted list when you start a line with an asterisk (*), a hyphen (-), or a greater than symbol (>) followed by a space or a tab. Likewise, it creates a numbered list when you start a line with a number followed by a period or a tab.

You can control the formatting that happens automatically as you type by placing or removing checkmarks.

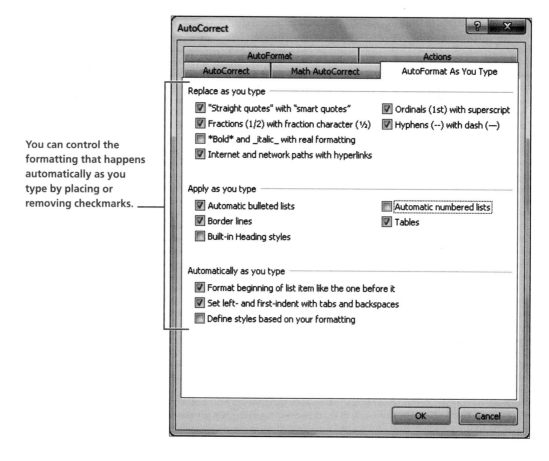

Turn On Automatic Numbering

In this exercise, you will turn on the option that automatically creates a numbered list when you begin a sentence with a number.

1. Click the **File** tab and then click the **Options** tab at the bottom of the Navigation pane.

2. Click **Proofing** on the left and then click the **AutoCorrect Options** button.

3. Follow these steps to turn on automatic numbering:

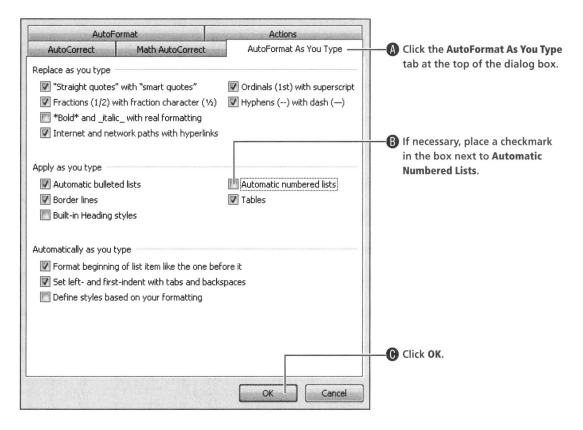

Ⓐ Click the **AutoFormat As You Type** tab at the top of the dialog box.

Ⓑ If necessary, place a checkmark in the box next to **Automatic Numbered Lists**.

Ⓒ Click **OK**.

4. Click **OK** again in the Word Options dialog box to close it.

5. Click the **Save** 🖫 button and leave the document **open** for the next exercise.

2.7 Copying and Moving Text

Video Lesson labyrinthelab.com/videos

FROM THE KEYBOARD

Ctrl+C to copy
Ctrl+X to cut
Ctrl+V to paste

Cut, Copy, and Paste allow you to copy and move text within a document or between documents. The Cut, Copy, and Paste commands are conveniently located on the Ribbon in the Clipboard command group at the left side of the Home tab.

The following table describes these commands.

QUICK REFERENCE	USING CUT, COPY, AND PASTE	
Command	**Description**	**How to Issue the Command**
Cut	The Cut command removes selected text from its original location and places it on the Clipboard.	Click the Cut ✂ button.
Copy	The Copy command places a copy of selected text on the Clipboard, but it also leaves the text in the original location.	Click the Copy 📋 button.
Paste	The Paste command pastes the most recently cut or copied text into the document at the insertion point location.	Click the Paste 📋 button.

Working with the Clipboard

The Clipboard lets you collect multiple items and paste them into another location in the current document or into a different document. It must be visible on the screen to collect the items; otherwise, only one item at a time is saved for pasting. The Clipboard can hold up to 24 items. When the items you cut or copy exceed 24, the Clipboard automatically deletes the oldest item(s).

The dialog box launcher 🔲 that displays the Clipboard task pane is located on the Home tab of the Ribbon.

The following illustration points out the main features of the Clipboard.

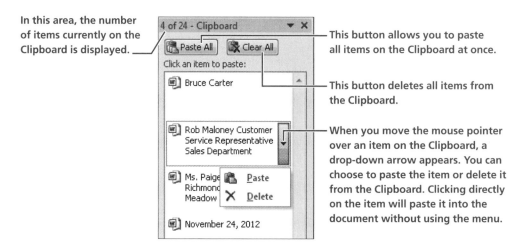

In this area, the number of items currently on the Clipboard is displayed.

This button allows you to paste all items on the Clipboard at once.

This button deletes all items from the Clipboard.

When you move the mouse pointer over an item on the Clipboard, a drop-down arrow appears. You can choose to paste the item or delete it from the Clipboard. Clicking directly on the item will paste it into the document without using the menu.

Use Cut, Copy, and Paste

In this exercise, you will move and copy information and work with the Clipboard.

1. If necessary, choose **Home→Paragraph→Show/Hide** ¶ from the Ribbon to display the formatting marks.

Copy and Paste Using the Clipboard

2. Choose **Home→Clipboard→dialog box launcher** 🔲 from the Ribbon.

3. Tap Ctrl + Home, then position the **mouse pointer** in the margin to the left of the date and then **click** to select the line.

4. Choose **Home→Clipboard→Copy** 📋 from the Ribbon.

5. Tap Ctrl + End to move the insertion point to the bottom of the document.

6. Follow these steps to paste the date at the bottom of the document:

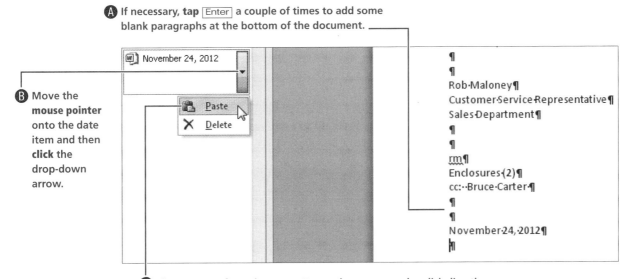

Ⓐ If necessary, **tap** Enter a couple of times to add some blank paragraphs at the bottom of the document.

Ⓑ Move the **mouse pointer** onto the date item and then **click** the drop-down arrow.

Ⓒ Choose **Paste** from the menu. Remember, you can also click directly on the item without using the menu and drop-down arrow.

Notice the Paste Options smart tag that popped up at the bottom of the pasted text.

7. Click the **smart tag** to view its menu and then click anywhere in the document to close the menu.

8. Tap Esc to dismiss the smart tag.

> If you don't tap Esc, the button will disappear on its own.

9. Click **Undo** 🔄 to undo the paste.

Move the Inside Address

10. **Scroll up** to the top of the letter, position the **mouse pointer** in the margin to the left of the first line of the inside address, and then **drag** to select all four lines.

11. **Tap** Ctrl+X to cut the text.
Notice that using the keyboard shortcut to cut text also puts the item on the Clipboard.

12. **Tap** Ctrl+End to move the insertion point to the bottom of the document.

13. Click the **inside address** on the Clipboard to paste it at the insertion point.

14. Click **Undo** 🔄 twice to undo the move and place the address back at the top of the letter.

15. Click the **Close** ☒ button on the Clipboard task pane.

16. Click the **Save** 💾 button to save the changes.

Editing with Drag and Drop

Video Lesson labyrinthelab.com/videos

Drag and drop produces the same result as cut, copy, and paste. It is efficient for moving or copying text a short distance within the same page. You select the text you wish to move and then drag it to the desired destination. If you press and hold Ctrl while dragging, the text is copied to the destination.

Drag and drop does not place the selection on the Clipboard.

DEVELOP YOUR SKILLS 2.7.2
Use Drag and Drop

In this exercise, you will use drag and drop to move and copy text.

1. Make sure there are a couple of **blank lines** at the bottom of your document.

2. If necessary, **scroll** so that you can see both the bottom of the document and the *Rob Maloney* line in the signature block.

Drag and Drop Move

3. **Select** the *Rob Maloney* line, and then **release** the mouse button.

4. Place the **mouse pointer** in the highlighted text.
The pointer now looks like a white arrow.

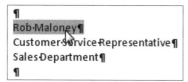

5. Press and hold the mouse button, and follow these steps to move the text:

¶
Rob·Maloney¶
Customer·Service·Representative¶
Sales·Department¶
¶
¶
rm¶
Enclosures·(2)¶
cc:··Bruce·Carter·¶
¶
¶

Ⓐ Drag down to the bottom of the document, and when you do so, the mouse pointer has a small rectangle at the bottom indicating you are in drag-and-drop mode. _____

Ⓑ You will also see a dotted insertion point that travels with the mouse pointer. Position it at the **bottom** of the document. _____

Ⓒ Release the mouse button to complete the move.

Now you will undo the move and repeat the process, but this time you'll copy the text.

6. Click the **Undo** 🔄 button to undo the move.

Drag and Drop Copy

7. Make sure the *Rob Maloney* line is still selected.

8. Place the **mouse pointer** inside the selected text, **press and hold** the Ctrl key and **drag** the text to the bottom of the document, **release** the mouse button, and then **release** the Ctrl key.
Holding the Ctrl key while dragging is what causes the action to be a copy instead of a move. For this reason, you must release the mouse button before the Ctrl key; otherwise, the action will become a move.

9. Click **Undo** 🔄 to undo the copy.

10. Leave the document **open** for the next exercise.
Soon you will learn to switch between documents so you can copy information from one document to another.

2.8 Switching Between Documents

Video Lesson   labyrinthelab.com/videos

There are several techniques for switching between documents. In the next exercise, you  will use the taskbar at the bottom of the screen for switching documents. When you have multiple documents open, they will appear as buttons on the taskbar. Clicking a button displays that document in the foreground. In the following illustration, Daniels Letter is the active document. The active document button is lighter than the others.

Viewing Open Documents on the Taskbar

When several documents are open at the same time, they may share one taskbar button. A small image of each open document displays on the screen when you hover the mouse pointer over the taskbar button. You can click the image to display the full document on the screen.

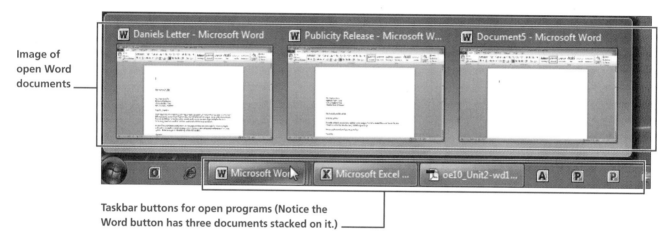

Image of open Word documents

Taskbar buttons for open programs (Notice the Word button has three documents stacked on it.)

 Your buttons may be different from the ones shown in the preceding illustration, depending on which program buttons are displayed on your computer's taskbar.

DEVELOP YOUR SKILLS 2.8.1
Switch and Copy Between Documents

In this exercise, you will copy and paste between two documents, using the taskbar buttons to switch between the documents.

1. **Open** the Publicity Release document in the Lesson 02 folder.

2. Follow these steps to switch to the Daniels Letter:

Ⓐ Hover the **mouse pointer** over the Microsoft Word taskbar button to display small images of the documents.

Ⓑ Click the **Daniels Letter**.

Copy and Paste the Inside Address

3. **Select** the four lines of the inside address and **tap** ⌷Ctrl⌷+⌷C⌷ to copy the text.

4. Hover the **mouse pointer** over the Microsoft Word taskbar button again and **click** the image of the Publicity Release document to switch to it.

5. Select the **first three lines**, as shown to the right.

6. **Tap** ⌷Ctrl⌷+⌷V⌷ to paste the address over the selected text in this document.

> YOUR·NAME¶
> ADDRESS¶
> CITY,·STATE··ZIP¶

Paste the Sales Manager's Name Multiple Times

7. Using the **taskbar**, switch back to the Daniels Letter, and then **select** *Bruce Carter* in the second line of the second paragraph.

8. **Tap** ⌷Ctrl⌷+⌷C⌷ to copy his name.

9. Using the **taskbar** button, **switch** back to the Publicity Release document.

10. **Select** *SALES MANAGER* in the salutation and then **tap** ⌷Ctrl⌷+⌷V⌷ to paste *Bruce Carter*. *Notice that the salutation does not look exactly right; it should be a title with a last name. You will fix that in just a moment.*

11. **Select** *SALES MANAGER* in the first paragraph and then **tap** ⌷Ctrl⌷+⌷V⌷ to paste *Bruce Carter* again.

Once you have copied text, you can paste it multiple times without copying the text again.

12. **Double-click** *Bruce* in the salutation and type **Mr**.

13. **Select** and **copy** *Paige Daniels* at the top of the letter; **paste** it over *YOUR NAME* at the bottom of the document.

Save and Close the Publicity Release Document

14. **Save** 💾 the changes you made in this document and then **close** it.

15. **Save** 💾 the changes to Daniels Letter, but leave it **open** for the next exercise.

2.9 Using Page Layout Options

Video Lesson   labyrinthelab.com/videos

The three most commonly used layout options are margins, page orientation, and paper size. All of these are located in the Page Setup group on the Page Layout tab of the Ribbon.

Setting Margins

Margins determine the amount of white space between the text and the edge of the paper. You can set margins for the entire document, a section, or for selected text. The Margins gallery displays preset top, bottom, left, and right margins. The Custom Margins option at the bottom of the gallery opens the Page Setup dialog box.

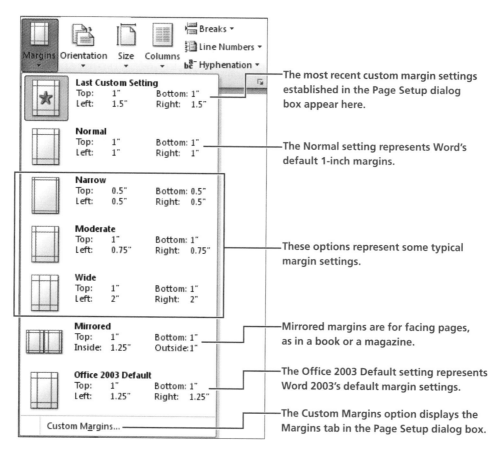

The most recent custom margin settings established in the Page Setup dialog box appear here.

The Normal setting represents Word's default 1-inch margins.

These options represent some typical margin settings.

Mirrored margins are for facing pages, as in a book or a magazine.

The Office 2003 Default setting represents Word 2003's default margin settings.

The Custom Margins option displays the Margins tab in the Page Setup dialog box.

QUICK REFERENCE	SETTING MARGINS
Task	**Procedure**
Change margins from the Margins gallery	■ Choose Page Layout→Page Setup→Margins from the Ribbon. ■ Choose predefined margin settings from the gallery.
Set custom margins	■ Choose Page Layout→Page Setup→Margins from the Ribbon. ■ Choose the Custom Margins command at the bottom of the gallery. ■ Enter settings for top, bottom, left, and right margins.

Set Page Layout Options

In this exercise, you will use the Margins gallery and the Page Setup dialog box to change the document's margins.

1. Choose **Page Layout→Page Setup→Margins** 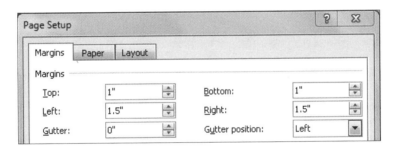 from the Ribbon to display Word's Margins gallery.

2. Choose **Narrow** from the gallery and observe the impact on your document.

3. Click the **Margins** button again to reopen the gallery and choose **Wide** to see how that affects the document.

4. Open the gallery again; change the margins back to the **Normal** (default) setting.

5. Click the **dialog box launcher** at the bottom-right corner of the Page Setup group to open the Page Setup dialog box.
   You can also open the dialog box using the Custom Margins command at the bottom of the Margins gallery.

6. If necessary, click the **Margins** tab at the top of the dialog box.
   Notice the options for changing the top, bottom, left, and right margins.

7. Use the **spinner controls** (up/down arrows) to change the left and right margins to **1.5 inches**.

8. Click **OK**; notice the change in your document's margins.

9. Click the **Margins** button to display the gallery and choose Normal.

10. **Save** the document and leave it **open** for the next exercise.

Setting the Page Orientation

Video Lesson   labyrinthelab.com/videos

The page orientation determines how the text is laid out on the paper. The options are vertically (Portrait) or horizontally (Landscape). The default orientation is Portrait. Some common uses for a landscape orientation include brochures, flyers, wide tables, and so forth. The Orientation options are located on the Page Layout tab of the Ribbon.

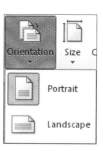

Setting the Paper Size

Most documents use the standard letter size paper. However, Word supports the use of many other paper sizes, including legal, and also allows you to create custom sizes.

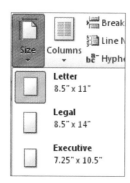

QUICK REFERENCE	SETTING PAGE ORIENTATION AND PAPER SIZE
Task	**Procedure**
Change the page orientation	■ Choose Page Layout→Page Setup→Orientation from the Ribbon.
	■ Choose the desired page orientation.
Change the paper size	■ Choose Page Layout→Page Setup→Size from the Ribbon.
	■ Choose the desired size from the menu, or choose the More Paper Sizes command to create a custom paper size.

DEVELOP YOUR SKILLS 2.9.2
Change the Orientation and Paper Size

In this exercise, you will experiment with the page orientation and paper size options.

View Landscape Orientation

1. If necessary, click the **Maximize** 🔲 button.

2. Choose **View→Zoom→One Page** 🔳 from the Ribbon.
   The page is currently in the default orientation of Portrait (vertical). Viewing the entire page allows you to see this clearly.

3. Choose **Page Layout→Page Setup→Orientation** 🔳 from the Ribbon.

4. Choose **Landscape** from the menu.
   The page layout changes to horizontal.

5. Click the **Orientation** button again and choose **Portrait** to change the page back to a vertical layout.

View Paper Size Options

6. Choose **Page Layout→Page Setup→Size** ⬚ from the Ribbon and switch to Legal.
   Notice the paper and envelope sizes available on the menu. The More Paper Sizes command at the bottom of the menu opens the Page Setup dialog box, where you can set a custom paper size if you wish.

7. Choose **Size** ⬚ again and switch back to **Letter**.

8. Choose **View→Zoom→100%** ⬚ from the Ribbon to have a larger view of the document.

9. **Save** ⬚ the document and leave it **open** for the next exercise.

2.10 Working with Combined Print and Print Preview

Video Lesson   <u>labyrinthelab.com/videos</u>

In Word 2010, the Print and Print Preview commands have been combined and are available in Backstage view. The left section is all about the printer and the current page layout options, while the right section is a preview of your document that shows how it will look when printed. You can experiment with different options and see the results immediately.

To display the Print options and Print Preview, choose File→Print.

You can no longer edit while previewing a document.

These options allow you to choose a different printer, view
the printer properties, and set the number of copies to print.

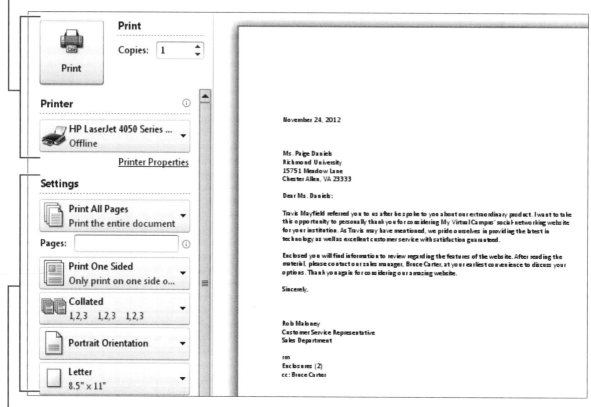

These options allow you to change various page layout options
and see the proposed change on the right in the preview section.

Experiment with Print and Print Preview

In this exercise, you will set printing and page layout options and preview the results.

1. Choose **File→Print**.

Explore Print Options

2. Follow these steps to print multiple copies of the current page:

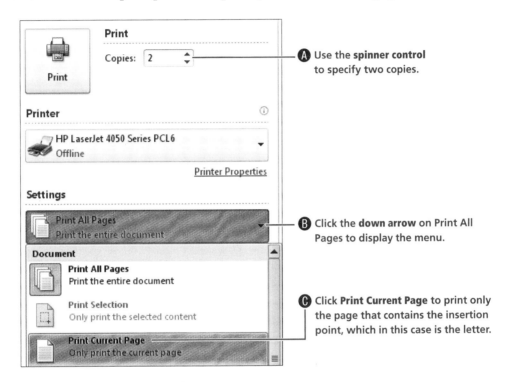

Ⓐ Use the **spinner control** to specify two copies.

Ⓑ Click the **down arrow** on Print All Pages to display the menu.

Ⓒ Click **Print Current Page** to print only the page that contains the insertion point, which in this case is the letter.

Preview Page Setting Changes

3. Follow these steps to preview the document with a different margin setting:

Ⓐ Click the **down arrow** on the Normal Margins setting.

Ⓑ Choose **Office 2003 Default**.

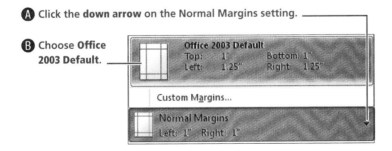

Notice the difference in the margins in the preview.

4. Switch back to the **Normal** margin setting.

5. Change the Orientation to **Landscape** and preview the change in the document.

6. Switch back to the **Portrait** orientation.

7. Click the **File** tab to close Backstage view and return to the document.

8. **Save** and **close** the document.

2.11 Concepts Review

Concepts Review   labyrinthelab.com/word10

To check your knowledge of the key concepts introduced in this lesson, complete the Concepts Review quiz by going to the URL listed above. If your classroom is using Labyrinth eLab, you may complete the Concepts Review quiz from within your eLab course.

Reinforce Your Skills

Create a Block-Style Letter

In this exercise, you will practice using traditional spacing for a business letter and letting Word Wrap and AutoComplete take effect. You should control the AutoCorrect feature as needed.

1. If necessary, **tap** Ctrl + N to start a new blank document.

2. Use the **Show/Hide ¶** button to display formatting marks.

3. Select the **paragraph symbol**, change the line spacing to **1.0**, and then **remove** the space after paragraphs. (You will need to open the menu twice to do this.)

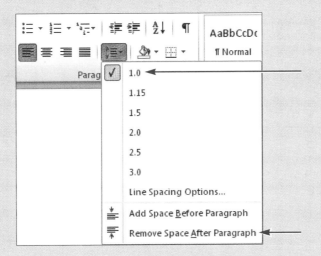

4. **Type** the following letter, **tapping** Enter wherever you see a paragraph symbol. Notice the five paragraph symbols at the top of the document. They position the date at approximately 2 inches from the top of the page.

```
¶
¶
¶
¶
¶
January·11,·2012¶
¶
¶
¶
Ms.·Courtney·Thompson¶
Service·Manager¶
Statesboro·Software·Services¶
810·Ivanhoe·Way¶
Statesboro,·GA·30458¶
¶
Dear·Ms.·Thompson:¶
¶
I·would·like·to·take·this·opportunity·to·thank·you·for·your·excellent·customer·service.·You·were·patient,·
courteous,·and·very·helpful.·The·installation·assistance·you·provided·was·invaluable.¶
¶
I·have·already·put·your·program·to·goo·d·use.·As·you·know,·application·programs·can·boost·personal·
productivity.·Your·program·allows·me·to·manage·my·business·much·more·effectively.·I·am·enclosing·the·
$45·fee·you·requested.·Please·send·me·a·receipt·and·a·catalog.¶
¶
Sincerely,¶
¶
¶
¶
Blake·Evans¶
Administrative·Assistant¶
¶
be¶
Enclosure¶
```

5. Position the **insertion point** just in front of the sentence starting *I am enclosing the $45*, and **tap** Enter twice to create a new paragraph.

6. Position the **insertion point** at the end of the second paragraph, just in front of the paragraph symbol.

7. **Tap** Delete twice to remove the two paragraph symbols separating the new paragraph from the following paragraph.

8. If necessary, **tap** the Spacebar to insert a space between the combined sentences.

9. Position the **insertion point** at the end of the first paragraph before the paragraph mark, and **tap** the Spacebar if there is no space at the end of the sentence.

10. **Type** this sentence: **I also appreciate the overnight delivery.**

11. Add an **envelope**, without a return address, to the top of the letter.

12. **Save** the letter in the Lesson 02 folder, name it **rs-Thompson Letter**, and then **close** it.

Use the Clipboard and Drag and Drop

In this exercise, you will open a document from your file storage location and use the Clipboard to rearrange paragraphs. You will use drag and drop to move blocks of text.

1. **Open** the rs-Professional Contacts document in the Lesson 02 folder.
   Notice that the document contains a list of professional contacts. In the next few steps, you will use the Clipboard to reorganize the contacts by profession: all the attorneys will be grouped together, followed by the designers, and then the bookkeepers.

2. Choose **Home→Clipboard→dialog box launcher** ⌐ from the Ribbon to display the Clipboard.

3. If necessary, click the **Clear All** button to clear the Clipboard.

4. **Select** the first attorney contact, *David Roberts, Attorney,* by clicking in front of the contact in the left margin.
   This will select the entire paragraph, including the paragraph mark.

5. Choose **Home→Clipboard→Cut** ✂ from the Ribbon.
   The item appears on the Clipboard.

6. **Select** the next attorney, *Lisa Wilson,* and **Cut** ✂ it to the Clipboard.

7. **Cut** the remaining attorney contacts to the Clipboard. Use **Undo** ↺ if you make a mistake. However, be careful because even if you use Undo, the item you cut will remain on the Clipboard.

8. Now **Cut** ✂ the designer contacts to the Clipboard.
   The bookkeeper contacts should now be grouped together in the document.

9. Click the **Paste All** button on the Clipboard to paste the attorney and designer contacts.
   Notice that the contacts are pasted in the order they were cut, thus grouping the attorneys together and the designers together.

Create Headings

10. Click to place the **insertion point** in front of the first bookkeeper contact, and **tap** Enter twice to create blank lines.

11. Click the **blank line** above the first bookkeeper and type **Bookkeepers**.

12. Use this technique to create headings for attorneys and designers.

Use Drag and Drop

13. Select the *Attorneys* heading, the four attorneys, and the blank line below by **dragging** in the left margin and then **releasing** the mouse button.

14. Position the **mouse pointer** on the selection, and **drag up** until the dotted insertion point is just in front of the Bookkeepers heading.

15. **Release** the mouse button to move the attorneys block above the bookkeepers.

16. Now move the designers above the bookkeepers.

17. **Close** the Clipboard, and then **save** and **close** the file.

Edit a Document

In this exercise, you will edit a document that is marked up for changes.

1. Choose **File→Open**.

2. **Open** the rs-Maine document in the Lesson 02 folder.
   You will edit this document during this exercise. Notice that this document contains formatting that you have not yet learned about. For example, the title is centered and bold, and the paragraphs are formatted with double line spacing. This document is already formatted like this because it is a report.

   - If only one or two characters require deletion, then position the **insertion point** in front of the character(s) and use Delete to remove them.
   - If one or more words require deletion, then select the text and use Delete to remove the selected text.
   - If a word or phrase needs to be replaced with another word or phrase, then select the desired text and type the replacement text.
   - Use **Undo** if you make mistakes.

3. When you have finished, **save** the changes and **close** the document.

MAINE – THE PINE TREE STATE

Maine is recognized as one of the most ~~healthy~~ *healthful* states in the nation with *summer* temperatures

averaging 70°F and winter temperatures averaging 20°F. It has 3,~~7~~*5*00 miles of coastline, is about

320 miles long and 210 miles wide, with a total area of 33,215 square miles or about as big as all

of the other five New England States combined. It comprises 16 counties with 22 cities, 424

towns, 51 plantations, and 416 unorganized townships. Aroostook county is so large (6,453

square miles) that it covers an area greater than the combined size of Connecticut *and Rhode Island*.

Maine abounds in natural assets—542,629 acres of state and national parks, including the

92-mile Allagash Wilderness Waterway, Acadia National Park (second most visited national

park in the United States), and Baxter State Park (location of Mt. Katahdin and the northern end

of the Appalachian Trail). Maine has one mountain ~~which~~ *that* is approximately one mile high—Mt.

Katahdin (5,268 ft. above sea level) and also claims America's first chartered city: York, 1641.

Maine's blueberry crop is the largest ~~blueberry crop~~ in the nation—98% of the low-bush

blueberries. Potatoes rank third in acreage and third in production nationally. Maine is nationally

famed for its shellfish; over 46 million pounds of ~~shellfish~~ *lobster* *in the United States* were harvested in 1997. The total of

all shellfish and fin fish harvested was approximately 237 million pounds with a total value of

$273 million *in 1997* ~~during the 1997 fishing season.~~

Apply Your Skills

Create a Modified Block-Style Letter

In this exercise, you will practice the skills needed to create a modified block-style letter. You'll turn on the ruler to ensure the correct spacing for the date, the complimentary close, and the signature block.

1. **Start** a new blank document.
   You will create an AutoCorrect entry for Back Bay Users Group to use in your letter.

2. Click the **File** tab and then click the **Options** button at the bottom of the Navigation pane.

3. In the Options window, choose **Proofing** from the menu on the left.

4. Click the **AutoCorrect Options** button.

5. When the AutoCorrect dialog box appears, type **bbug** in the **Replace** box.

6. Type **Back Bay Users Group** in the **With** box.

7. Click the **Add** button, and then click **OK** twice.

8. If necessary, click the **View Ruler** 🔲 button at the top of the vertical scroll bar to display the ruler.

9. Create the **modified block-style** business letter shown in the illustration on the next page.

10. Follow these guidelines as you type your letter.
    - Change to **single-spacing** and remove the **after-paragraph spacing**.
    - Space down the proper distance from the top of the page.
    - Use ⌐Tab¬ to align the date, closing, and signature block at **3 inches** on the ruler. (You'll need to **tap** ⌐Tab¬ six times to indent the lines at 3 inches.)
    - Use correct spacing between paragraphs.
    - Use your **AutoCorrect** shortcut in the first paragraph, rather than typing Back Bay Users Group.

```
                              Today's Date




Mrs. Suzanne Lee
8445 South Princeton Street
Chicago, IL 60628


Dear Mrs. Lee:

Thank you for your interest in the Back Bay Users Group. We will be holding an orientation for new
members on the first Thursday in April at our headquarters.

Please let us know if you can attend by calling the phone number on this letterhead. Or, if you prefer,
you may respond in writing or via email.


                              Sincerely,



                              Jack Bell
                              Membership Chair


xx
```

11. **Save** 💾 the letter to the Lesson 02 folder on your file storage location as **as-Lee Letter**.

12. **Hide** the ruler using the same button you used to display it.

13. **Delete** the AutoCorrect entry you created in this exercise.

14. **Preview** the letter, then preview how it would look in Landscape orientation with **Narrow** margins.

15. Restore to **Portrait** orientation and **Normal** margins.

16. **Print** the letter if your computer is connected to a printer, and then **save** and **close** the document.

APPLY YOUR SKILLS 2.2

Use the Clipboard and Drag and Drop

In this exercise, you will use the Clipboard and the drag-and-drop technique to rearrange items in a list.

1. **Open** as-Animals in the Lesson 02 folder in your file storage location.

2. Open the **Clipboard**, and use the **Clear All** button, if necessary, to empty it.

3. Use the **Home→Clipboard→Cut** ✂ button to place all the animals on the Clipboard, and then cut all the vegetables to the Clipboard.

4. Position the **insertion point** below the list of minerals, and then use the **Paste All** button to paste the animals and vegetables back in the document.

5. Use the ⌷Enter⌷ key to put two blank lines between groups and an extra blank line above the minerals, and then **type** an appropriate title at the top of each group.

6. Use **drag and drop** to arrange the groups in this order: Animals, Vegetables, Minerals. Remember, when selecting the text, include the blank line below the group.

7. **Save** 🖫 the file and **close** it.

Edit a Document

In this exercise, you will use your editing skills to make specified changes to a letter.

1. **Open** the as-Wilson Letter document in the Lesson 02 folder in your file storage location.

2. **Edit** the document, as shown in the illustration at the end of this exercise.

3. Use ⌷Enter⌷ to push the entire document down, so that the date is positioned at approximately the **1-inch** mark on the vertical ruler.

4. If necessary, use ⌷Tab⌷ to move the date, complimentary close, and signature block to the **3-inch** position on the ruler. This will convert the letter from block style to modified block style.

5. When you finish, **save** 🖫 the changes, **print** the letter, and **close** the document.

Today's Date

~~Ms. Cynthia Wilson~~ Mr. Roosevelt Jackson
~~118 Upper Terrace~~ 8 Spring Street
~~Freehold, NJ 08845~~ Martinville, NJ 08836

Dear ~~Ms. Wilson~~:
        Mr. Jackson
                                                                    back
Thank you for your recent letter concerning back injuries in your office. Yes, ⌄injuries are a common problem for office workers today. It was estimated by the U. S. Bureau of Labor Statistics that in one year over ~~490~~,000 employees took time from work due to back injuries.
                                        580

Encourage your office employees to make certain their work surface is at a ~~suitable~~ height. They should also be encouraged to take frequent breaks from their desks.   comfortable

Please
~~Feel free to~~ contact my office if you would like more information.

Sincerely,

Elaine Boudreau
Ergonomics Specialist

Critical Thinking &
Work-Readiness Skills

In the course of working through the following Microsoft Office-based Critical Thinking exercises, you will also be utilizing various work-readiness skills, some of which are listed next to each exercise. Go to labyrinthelab.com/ workreadiness to learn more about the work-readiness skills.

2.1 Create a Business Letter

WORK-READINESS SKILLS APPLIED

- Writing
- Serving clients/ customers
- Organizing and maintaining information

Stefanie Bentley, the marketing assistant for My Virtual Campus, has received an email from Mary Jones, the student life coordinator from Magnolia College (3000 College Lane, Anywhere, Iowa 22222) asking what's different about the My Virtual Campus service compared to other similar services. Write a response in business letter format stating that My Virtual Campus has the most flexible set of solutions and that you can demonstrate these solutions in an online meeting. Suggest a time and date two weeks from today, and mention that you have enclosed a brochure. Save the letter as **ct-Magnolia** to your Lesson 02 folder. Close the file.

2.2 Use AutoCorrect and AutoFormat

WORK-READINESS SKILLS APPLIED

- Writing
- Serving clients/ customers
- Applying technology to a task

After two weeks with no response from Mary at Magnolia College, Stefanie decides to send a follow-up letter. Create another business letter addressed to Mary (her title and contact details shown above) asking for confirmation that she received your earlier letter and suggesting another time for a meeting. Configure Word's AutoCorrect options to automatically replace **mvc** with *My Virtual Campus* and test it to make sure *mvc* is automatically corrected. Save your document to your Lesson 02 folder as **ct-Follow Up**. Delete the custom AutoCorrect entry so other students can perform this exercise on the same computer later.

2.3 Combine and Switch Between Documents

WORK-READINESS SKILLS APPLIED

- Thinking creatively
- Making decisions
- Organizing and maintaining information

Stefanie decides to blend content from multiple documents so she has a single tool she can use for marketing purposes. Open the files ct-MVC Description Rev 1 and ct-MVC Description Rev 2 from the Lesson 02 folder. Cut, paste, drag and drop, and use any other editing techniques to combine the two descriptions into a single, complete description of My Virtual Campus. You will have to decide which document will contain the updated edits. Save that document to your Lesson 02 folder as **ct-MVC Description Final**.

Creating a Memorandum and a Press Release

LEARNING OBJECTIVES

After studying this lesson, you will be able to:

- Insert dates and symbols
- Insert and delete page breaks
- Work with proofreading tools
- Use Research options
- Work with formatting features
- Search using the Navigation pane and Find and Replace
- Work with hyperlinks and bookmarks

In this lesson, you will expand on the basic Word skills you've developed. You will create a memo and a press release and then apply character formatting. You will also get experience with Word's proofing and editing tools, including Spelling & Grammar check. Finally, you will find synonyms in Word's thesaurus and explore other research options.

Preparing a Memorandum

My Virtual Campus continues to grow and is constantly adding the newest advancements in technology. Brett Martin is the public relations representative, and she regularly issues press releases to  members and potential customers, trumpeting forthcoming upgrades. Brett creates a memorandum to which she attaches her latest press release announcing the launch of MyResume, which is being integrated into the website. Memorandums are used for internal communication within a company or organization, whereas business letters are used for external communication. Brett understands the importance of protecting the corporation's proprietary information, so she uses the appropriate trademark designations in her documents.

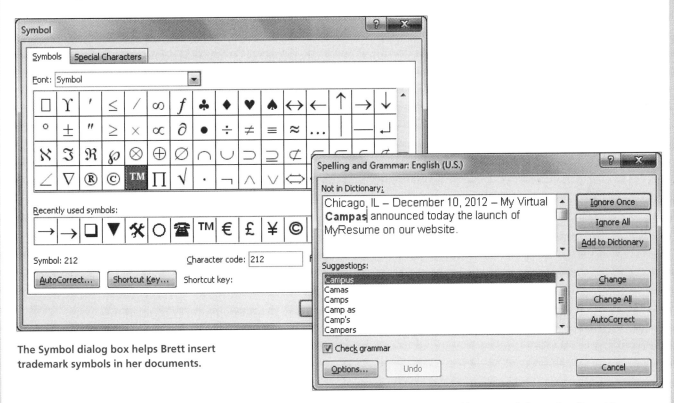

The Symbol dialog box helps Brett insert trademark symbols in her documents.

The Spelling and Grammar tool is a powerful proofreading aid.

3.1 Typing a Memorandum

Video Lesson labyrinthelab.com/videos

There are a variety of acceptable memorandum styles in use today. All memorandum styles contain the same elements but with varied formatting. The style shown in the following figure is a traditional memorandum style with minimal formatting.

The introduction includes headings such as Memo To: and From:. Use a double space between paragraphs, or use the new Microsoft spacing, which automatically adds space after a paragraph. This means you only need to tap Enter once between paragraphs.

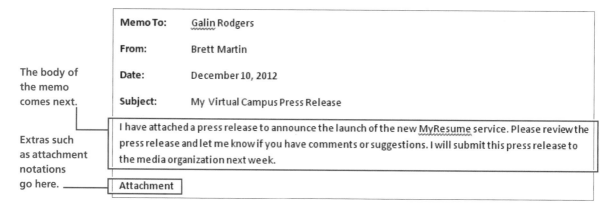

Introducing Default Tabs

The Tab key moves the insertion point to the nearest tab stop. In Word, the default tab stops are set every $1/2$ inch, thus the insertion point moves $1/2$ inch whenever you tap the Tab key. In this lesson, you will use Word's default tab settings.

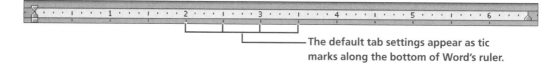

The default tab settings appear as tic marks along the bottom of Word's ruler.

 A quick way to turn the ruler on and off is to click the View Ruler button at the top of the scroll bar.

Inserting and Formatting the Date

You use the Insert→Text→Insert Date and Time 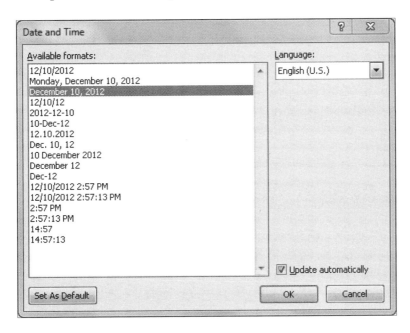 command on the Ribbon to display the Date and Time dialog box. Word lets you insert the current date in a variety of formats. For example, the date could be inserted as 12/10/12, December 10, 2012, or 10 December 2012.

FROM THE KEYBOARD

Alt + Shift + D
to insert a date

The Update Automatically Option

You can insert the date and time as text or as a field. Inserting the date as text has the same effect as typing the date into a document. Fields, however, are updated whenever a document is saved or printed. For example, imagine you create a document on December 10, 2012, and you insert the date as a field. If you open the document the next day, the date will automatically change to December 11, 2012. The date and time are inserted as fields whenever the Update Automatically box is checked, as shown here.

DEVELOP YOUR SKILLS 3.1.1

Set Up a Memo and Insert the Date

In this exercise, you will create a memo and insert the date automatically. You will also try out Word's 1.15 line spacing and the extra space following paragraphs.

Set Up a Memo

1. **Start** a new blank document. Make sure the Word window is **maximized** ▣.

2. If necessary, click the **View Ruler** 🔲 button at the top of the vertical scroll bar to turn on the ruler.

3. **Tap** [Enter] twice to space down to approximately 2 inches from the top of the page (1-inch mark on the vertical ruler).
   Using Word's default spacing, you don't have to tap [Enter] as many times as you did in the previous lesson to position the insertion point at 2 inches.

4. Type **Memo To:** and **tap** the Tab key.

   Notice that the insertion point moves to the next $^1/_2$-inch mark on the ruler.

5. If necessary, choose **Home→Paragraph→Show/Hide** ¶ from the Ribbon to display formatting marks.

   Notice the arrow formatting mark that represents the tab.

6. Type **Galin Rodgers** and **tap** Enter once.

   Notice that the word Galin has a red wavy underline, indicating it is not in Word's dictionary.

7. Type **From:** and **tap** Tab twice.

   It is necessary to Tab *twice to align the names. The first tab aligns the insertion point at the $^1/_2$-inch mark on the ruler; the second aligns the insertion point at the 1-inch position.*

8. Type **Brett Martin** and **tap** Enter once.

9. Type **Date:** and **tap** Tab twice.

Choose a Date Format and Insert the Date

10. Choose **Insert→Text→Insert Date and Time** 🗓 from the Ribbon to display the Date and Time dialog box.

11. Follow these steps to insert the date:

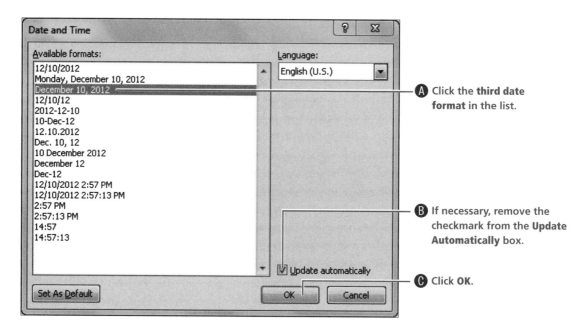

Leaving the Update Automatically box checked instructs Word to insert the date as a field, which means the original date would be lost if you opened and saved the document at a later date. In this instance, you do not want the date to change.

12. Choose **Home→Paragraph→Show/Hide** ¶ to turn off the paragraph marks.

13. Complete the remainder of the memorandum, as shown in the following illustration, using the [Tab] to align the text in the Subject line. Bear in mind that you only need to **tap** [Enter] once between paragraphs.

Memo To: Galin Rodgers

From: Brett Martin

Date: December 10, 2012

Subject: My Virtual Campus Press Release

I have attached a press release to announce the launch of the new MyResume service. Please review the press release and let me know if you have comments or suggestions. I will submit this press release to the media organization next week.

Attachment

---

14. Click the **View Ruler** button at the top of the scroll bar to turn off the ruler.

15. Click the **Save** button, and save the document in Lesson 03 folder as **Martin Memo**.

16. Leave the memorandum **open**, as you will modify it throughout this lesson.

Inserting Symbols

Video Lesson   labyrinthelab.com/videos

Word lets you insert a variety of symbols, typographic characters, and international characters not found on the keyboard. You insert symbols via the Symbol dialog box. The following illustration shows how you access the Symbol dialog box. You can also use shortcut key combinations to insert certain symbols; for example, type (c), (r), or (tm) to insert the copyright, registered trademark, or trademark symbols, respectively.

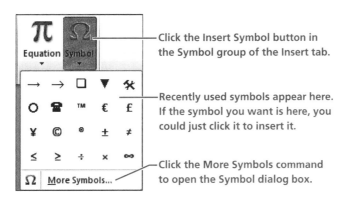

Click the Insert Symbol button in the Symbol group of the Insert tab.

Recently used symbols appear here. If the symbol you want is here, you could just click it to insert it.

Click the More Symbols command to open the Symbol dialog box.

The Special Characters tab displays commonly used special characters, such as the registered trademark (®) symbol and various punctuation symbols.

You can choose from several fonts, each displaying a different set of characters in the dialog box. Some fonts, such as Wingdings, contain interesting and fun symbols.

You can look up or set an AutoCorrect entry (or a keyboard shortcut) that may be used to insert a symbol rather than opening this dialog box.

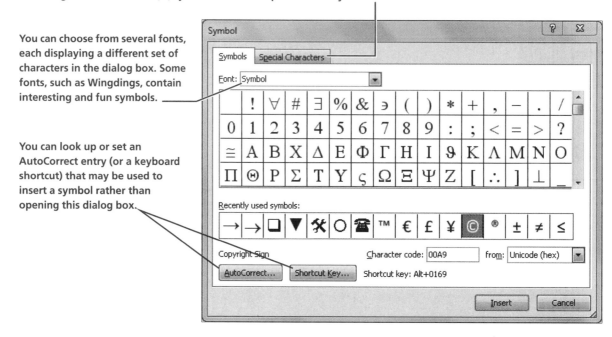

DEVELOP YOUR SKILLS 3.1.2

Insert Symbols

In this exercise, you will add a trademark symbol and a registered trademark symbol to your document.

1. Position the **insertion point** to the right of *My Virtual Campus* on the *Subject:* line.

2. Click **Insert→Symbols→Insert Symbol** Ω from the Ribbon, and choose the **More Symbols** command at the bottom of the menu.

3. When the Symbol dialog box appears, click the **Special Characters** tab.

4. Choose the **registered trademark symbol** (an R inside a circle), and then click the **Insert** button.
   The ® symbol is inserted in the document, and the Symbol dialog box remains open. Word leaves the dialog box open in case you wish to insert additional symbols.

5. Position the **insertion point** to the right of *MyResume* in the main paragraph.
   You may need to drag the dialog box out of the way in order to see the word. To do that, position the mouse pointer on the blue title bar at the top of the dialog box, press and hold the mouse button, drag the dialog box out of the way, and then release the mouse button.

6. Click the **trademark** (™) symbol from Special Characters and then click **Insert**.
   The trademark (™) symbol indicates that a company claims a phrase or icon as its trademark but has not received the federal protection accompanying the registered trademark (®) symbol.

7. Click the **Symbols** tab in the Symbol dialog box, and choose different fonts from the Font list to see other sets of symbols.

8. When you finish experimenting, click the **Close** button to close the dialog box.

9. Click the **Save** 💾 button to save the changes.

3.2 Working with Page Breaks

Video Lesson   labyrinthelab.com/videos

If you are typing text and the insertion point reaches the bottom of a page, Word automatically breaks the page and begins a new page. This is known as an automatic page break. The location of automatic page breaks may change as text is added to or deleted from a document. Automatic page breaks are convenient when working with long documents that have continuously flowing text. For example, imagine you were writing a novel and you decided to insert a new paragraph in the middle of a chapter. With automatic page breaks, you could insert the paragraph and Word would automatically repaginate the entire chapter.

You force a page break by choosing Insert→Pages→Page Break 📄 from the Ribbon. A manual page break remains in place unless you remove it. You insert manual page breaks whenever you want to control the starting point of a new page.

FROM THE KEYBOARD

Ctrl+Enter to insert a page break

If you are working on a first draft or a document you suspect will go through revisions, it is not a good idea to insert manual page breaks because the pages will not repaginate correctly and you may end up with unwanted blank pages.

Removing Manual Page Breaks

In Draft view, a manual page break appears as a horizontal line, including the phrase *Page Break*. You can also see the page break line in Print Layout view if you turn on the Show/Hide feature. You can remove a manual page break by positioning the insertion point on the page break line and tapping Delete, as shown in the illustration to the right.

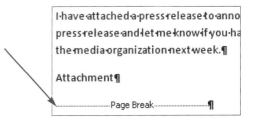

Displaying the Word Count

Microsoft Word tracks the number of words, pages, characters, paragraphs, and lines as you type them in a document. The number of words is displayed on the Word Count button on the Status bar; the other counts are available when you double-click the Word Count button.

You may need to count the number of words in a certain paragraph, a certain page, and so forth. To check these statistics, you need to first select the text; you can even select sections of text that are not connected to each other. The word count appears on the Status bar, which shows the number of selected words and the total number of words in the document. For example, a 42-word selection in a document that contains 60 words would display as 42/60.

Page: 1 of 2 | Words: 42/60 —— Word Count button on Status bar

Select nonadjacent sections by highlighting the first selection, holding down the Ctrl key, and then selecting the additional sections.

Work with Page Breaks

In this exercise, you will practice using manual page breaks. You will insert a page break, thereby creating a new page so you can copy and paste the press release information from another document into your new page.

Insert a Page Break

1. Make sure you are in **Print Layout** view. If you are not sure, click the **View** tab and choose **Print Layout** from the Document Views group at the left edge of the Ribbon. (If the button is highlighted, you are already in Print Layout view.)

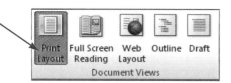

2. **Tap** [Ctrl]+[End] to position the insertion point at the bottom of the document and, if necessary, **tap** [Enter] to generate a blank line below the *Attachment* line.

3. Choose **Insert→Pages→Page Break** ⊟ from the Ribbon.

4. Select the body paragraph and view the **Word Count** button the Status bar.
   Notice that the numbers 42/60 represent the number of words selected and total number in the document.

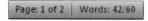

5. If necessary, **scroll** to see the bottom portion of page 1 and the top of page 2.

Remove the Page Break

6. **Scroll** up until the *Attachment* line is visible.

7. If necessary, click **Home→Paragraph→Show/Hide** ¶ to display formatting marks and see the page break.

8. **Click** to the left of the page break line, and tap [Delete].

9. Try **scrolling** down to the second page and you will see that it is gone.

Reinsert the Page Break

10. Check to see that the **insertion point** is just below the *Attachment* line, and **tap** [Ctrl]+[Enter] to reinsert the page break.
    This shortcut keystroke is useful when you use page breaks frequently.

11. Click **Home→Paragraph→Show/Hide** ¶ to hide the formatting marks.
    The insertion point should be positioned at the top of the second page.

Copy and Paste from Another Document

12. Click **File→Open** and, if necessary, navigate to your file storage location and **open** Press Release from the Lesson 03 folder.
    Notice that a number of phrases are flagged by the spelling checker (red wavy underlines) and grammar checker (green wavy underlines) in the document. You will take care of those in the next exercise.

13. In the Press Release document, **tap** Ctrl + A to select the entire document.

14. **Tap** Ctrl + C to copy the document.
    Now you will switch to your memo.

15. On the taskbar, click the **Martin Memo** button to switch back to that document.

16. Make sure your **insertion point** is at the top of page 2.

17. Choose **Home→Clipboard→Paste** from the Ribbon.
    The press release is pasted on page 2 of your document. Now you will switch back to the press release and close it.

18. Use the **taskbar** button to switch to Press Release.

19. Choose **File→Close** to close the file.
    The Martin Memo should now be in the foreground.

20. **Save** the file and leave it **open** for the next exercise.

3.3 Working with Proofreading Tools

Video Lesson labyrinthelab.com/videos

Word's powerful Spelling and Grammar tool helps you avoid embarrassing spelling and grammar errors. Whether you choose to use the default on-the-fly checking, where Word marks possible errors as you type, or you choose to save proofing tasks until you've completed your document content, these tools can help polish your writing. However, these tools are proofreading aids, not the final word. You still need to involve human judgment in a final round of proofing, such as making sure you don't overuse a particular word. The Thesaurus can aid in finding alternate words for you.

■ Spelling checker
■ Grammar checker
■ Research Task Pane

Using the Spelling Checker

Word checks a document for spelling errors by comparing each word to the contents of its built-in dictionary. Word also looks for double words such as *the the,* and a variety of capitalization errors. If you start the spelling checker in the middle of the document, when it reaches the end, a message appears asking if you want to go back and start spell checking from the beginning of the document.

Word can automatically check your spelling as you type. It flags spelling errors by underlining them with wavy red lines. You can correct a flagged error by right-clicking the error and choosing a suggested replacement word or other option from the menu that pops up.

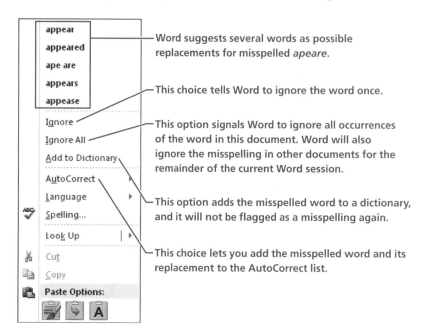

Word suggests several words as possible replacements for misspelled *apeare*.

This choice tells Word to ignore the word once.

This option signals Word to ignore all occurrences of the word in this document. Word will also ignore the misspelling in other documents for the remainder of the current Word session.

This option adds the misspelled word to a dictionary, and it will not be flagged as a misspelling again.

This choice lets you add the misspelled word and its replacement to the AutoCorrect list.

Working with Word's Dictionaries

The main Word dictionary contains thousands of common words; however, it may not include proper names, acronyms, technical terminology, and so forth. When you run the spelling checker and it comes across a word not found in the main dictionary, it marks the word as a possible spelling error. If that word is one that you use often in your writing, you can add it so the spelling checker recognizes it the next time and does not mark it as an error.

Dictionary Options

When the Suggest from Main Dictionary Only checkbox is unchecked, the spelling checker will search for words in the custom dictionaries; however, if that option is checked, it will only search the main dictionary. Adding a word during spell checking adds that word to a custom dictionary. The dictionary options are found on the Proofing page in the Word Options dialog box.

Choose whether Word includes suggestions from custom dictionaries or only the main dictionary.

Access the list of words added to the custom dictionaries.

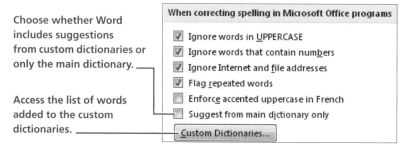

 The options you set for custom dictionaries in Microsoft Word apply to all Office programs.

Remove a Word from a Custom Dictionary

You may add a word to a custom dictionary and then realize it was a mistake. This is not a problem because you can remove it using the Custom Dictionaries dialog box. You simply open the custom dictionary, display the word list, and choose which word to delete.

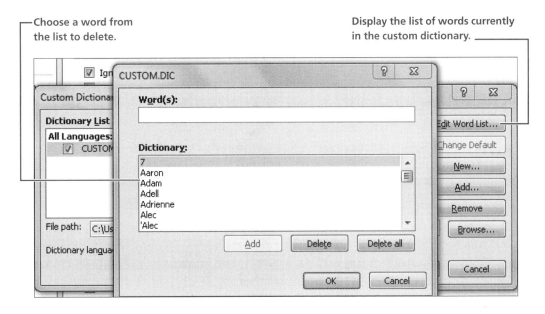

┌─Choose a word from the list to delete.

Display the list of words currently in the custom dictionary.─┐

Use Automatic Spelling Checker

In this exercise, you will use the Ignore All option on the spelling checker pop-up menu to remove the red underlines from all occurrences of the words MyResume. *You will also delete a repeated word.*

Spellcheck Using Ignore All

1. Notice that the word *MyResume* in the first line of page 2 has a wavy red underline. This word appears a number of times in the document.
   MyResume *is spelled correctly; it's just that it does not appear in Word's dictionary. As a result, Word flags it as a possible spelling error.*

2. Follow these steps to have the spelling checker ignore all occurrences of *MyResume* and thereby remove the wavy red underline wherever the term appears:

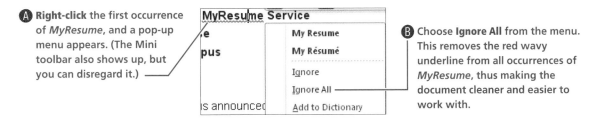

A **Right-click** the first occurrence of *MyResume*, and a pop-up menu appears. (The Mini toolbar also shows up, but you can disregard it.)

B Choose **Ignore All** from the menu. This removes the red wavy underline from all occurrences of *MyResume*, thus making the document cleaner and easier to work with.

Work with Double Word Errors

Word flagged a double word error in the first paragraph of the press release.

3. **Right-click** the word *our* with the wavy red line, and choose the **Delete Repeated Word** command from the menu.

4. **Save** 💾 your file and leave it **open** for the next exercise.

Using the Grammar Checker

Video Lesson labyrinthelab.com/videos

Word has a sophisticated grammar checker that can help you with your writing skills. Like the spelling checker, the grammar checker can check grammar as you type. The grammar checker flags errors by underlining them with wavy green lines. You can correct a flagged error by right-clicking the error and choosing a replacement phrase or other option from the pop-up menu. Be careful when using the grammar checker. It isn't perfect. There is no substitute for careful proofreading.

Grammar checking is active by default. Grammar checking options are available by clicking the File tab, then clicking the Options tab to display the Word Options window. You can enable or disable the feature by checking or unchecking the boxes shown in the figure to the right.

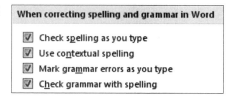

The Spelling and Grammar Dialog Box

FROM THE KEYBOARD

F7 to start the Spelling & Grammar check

Choose Review→Proofing→Spelling and Grammar 🔤 from the Ribbon to display the Spelling and Grammar dialog box. You may prefer to focus on your document's content and postpone proofing until you're done. You can use the Spelling and Grammar dialog box for that purpose.

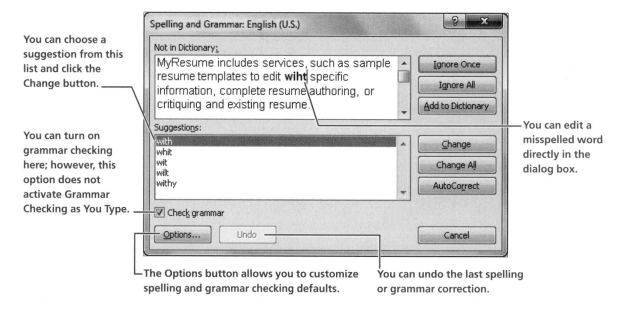

You can choose a suggestion from this list and click the Change button.

You can turn on grammar checking here; however, this option does not activate Grammar Checking as You Type.

You can edit a misspelled word directly in the dialog box.

The Options button allows you to customize spelling and grammar checking defaults.

You can undo the last spelling or grammar correction.

Use the Spelling and Grammar Dialog Box

In this exercise, you will make corrections to the Martin Memo using the Spelling and Grammar dialog box. If you do not see any text underlined in green, the grammar checking options are turned off on your computer. If you see the green grammar check lines in your document, follow the steps to turn the feature on anyway, so you will know where to locate the feature in the future.

1. Click the **File** tab and then click the **Options** tab to display the Word Options window.

2. Choose **Proofing** from the menu on the left.

3. Follow these steps to turn on grammar checking:

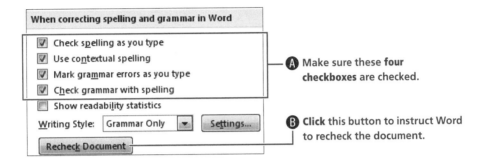

Ⓐ Make sure these **four checkboxes** are checked.

Ⓑ **Click** this button to instruct Word to recheck the document.

4. When the message box appears, choose **Yes** to dismiss the message, then click **OK** to close the window.
   Since you clicked Recheck Document, notice that MyResume *has wavy red lines again.*

5. Position the **insertion point** at the beginning of the first line on page 2.

6. Choose **Review→Proofing→Spelling and Grammar** ✔ from the Ribbon.
   The Spelling and Grammar dialog box appears, and MyResume *is noted as a possible spelling error.*

7. Click the **Add to Dictionary** button.
   You will delete MyResume *from the Custom Dictionary a little later in this exercise.*

8. The next error is a simple typo; the suggestion with is correct, so click the **Change** button.
   Now Word points out a possible grammatical error.

Use the Grammar Checker

9. Follow these steps to correct the grammatical error:

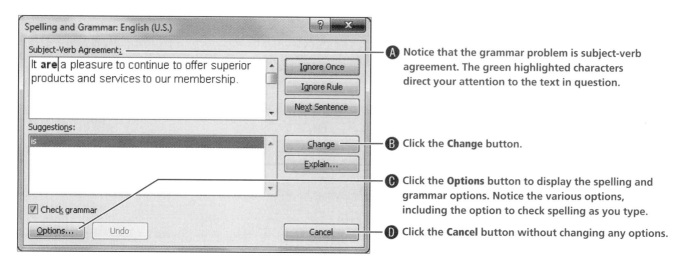

A Notice that the grammar problem is subject-verb agreement. The green highlighted characters direct your attention to the text in question.

B Click the **Change** button.

C Click the **Options** button to display the spelling and grammar options. Notice the various options, including the option to check spelling as you type.

D Click the **Cancel** button without changing any options.

10. The next error is a spelling error, and the suggestion *Delivery* is correct, so click the **Change** button.

11. Finish checking the rest of the press release using your own good judgment regarding what changes to make. When *Galin* is flagged, click the **Ignore Once** button.

12. When the message appears indicating that the spelling and grammar check is complete, click **OK**.

Remove a Word from the Custom Dictionary

You will now delete the name MyResume that you added to the dictionary earlier in this exercise.

13. Click **File→Options**.

14. Click the **Proofing** tab in the Navigation pane.

15. Follow these steps to display the word list in the Custom Dictionary:

A Click the **Custom Dictionaries** button.   **B** Click the **Edit Word List** button.

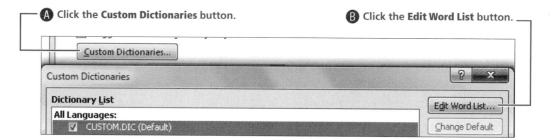

16. Follow these steps to delete *MyResume* from the word list:

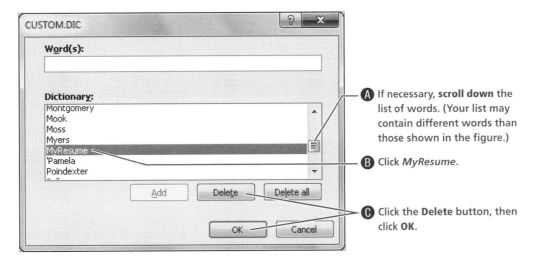

A If necessary, **scroll down** the list of words. (Your list may contain different words than those shown in the figure.)

B Click *MyResume*.

C Click the **Delete** button, then click **OK**.

17. Click **OK** two more times to close the remaining windows.

18. Save the file and leave it **open** for the next exercise.

Using the Thesaurus to Find a Synonym

Video Lesson labyrinthelab.com/videos

FROM THE KEYBOARD
Alt+click the word to look up for Thesaurus

A thesaurus contains words that have the same meaning as another word (synonyms). You can quickly see a list of synonyms for a word by simply right-clicking the word and choosing Synonyms. For a more extensive list with additional options, you can display the Research task pane by choosing Thesaurus from the bottom of the context menu or from the Proofing group on the Review tab of the Ribbon.

The Thesaurus also contains antonyms, which are words meaning the opposite of other words.

Using the Research Task Pane

The Research task pane goes beyond displaying a list of alternate words. As you know, a word can have different meanings depending upon the context in which it is used. For example, the word *certain* can be used to mean *sure, clear, particular,* or *some*. Using the Thesaurus in the Research task pane, you can look up those additional synonyms by clicking any word displayed in the results list.

In addition to displaying words from the Thesaurus, the Research task pane also provides access to other references, such as a dictionary, business and financial sites, and research sites.

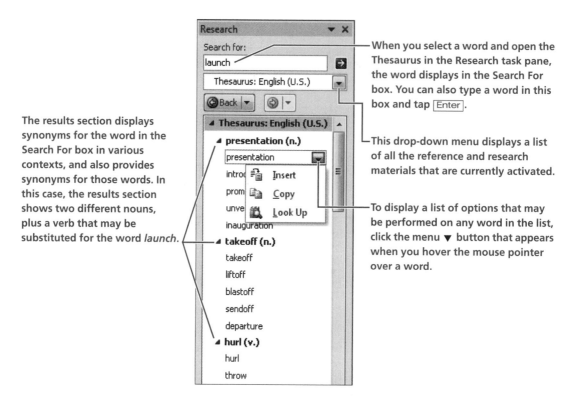

The results section displays synonyms for the word in the Search For box in various contexts, and also provides synonyms for those words. In this case, the results section shows two different nouns, plus a verb that may be substituted for the word *launch*.

When you select a word and open the Thesaurus in the Research task pane, the word displays in the Search For box. You can also type a word in this box and tap Enter.

This drop-down menu displays a list of all the reference and research materials that are currently activated.

To display a list of options that may be performed on any word in the list, click the menu ▼ button that appears when you hover the mouse pointer over a word.

Research Task Pane Options

Word already includes a long list of services in the Research task pane, though you may wish to add your favorites to the list. Certain services in the list are currently activated; however, you can choose which ones to activate and deactivate. When you perform a search, only the services that are currently activated will be researched.

DEVELOP YOUR SKILLS 3.3.3

Use the Thesaurus

In this exercise, you will use the context menu to replace a word with a synonym, and you will experiment with the Thesaurus in the Research task pane. Finally, you will activate and deactivate services in the Research Options.

Choose a Synonym from the Menu

1. **Scroll** to view the press release page.

2. **Right-click** the word *launch* in the first sentence of the *Announcement* paragraph.

3. Follow these steps to replace the word with a synonym:

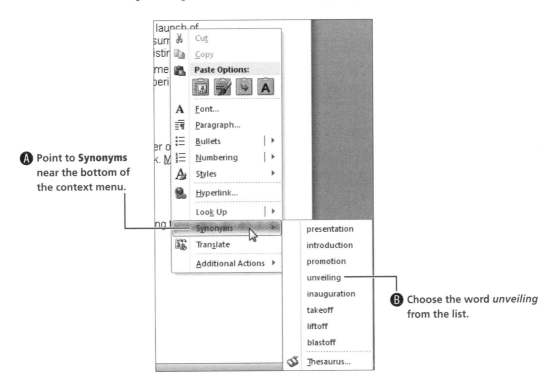

(A) Point to **Synonyms** near the bottom of the context menu.

(B) Choose the word *unveiling* from the list.

Notice that the word launch *in the first paragraph has been changed to* unveiling.

Look Up Synonyms in the Research Task Pane

4. Choose **Review→Proofing→Thesaurus** from the Ribbon.

5. Follow these steps to insert an alternate word for *unveiling*:

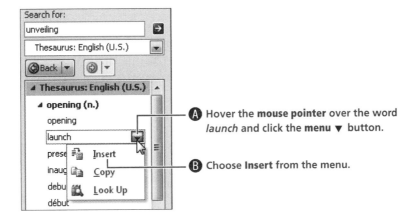

(A) Hover the **mouse pointer** over the word *launch* and click the **menu ▼** button.

(B) Choose **Insert** from the menu.

6. While the Research task pane is still displayed, **click** any word in the results section to view synonyms for that word.

Change a Research Option

7. Choose **Research Options** from the bottom of the Research task pane.

8. Click the **checkbox** next to Diccionario de la Real Academia Española.

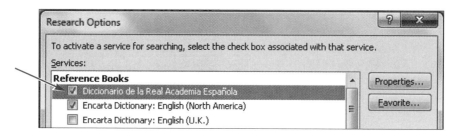

9. Before clicking OK, scroll down through the list to view the available services which may or may not be activated.
Please do not activate or deactivate services unless are instructed to do so in the classroom.

10. Click the **Thesaurus: English (U.S.) menu ▼** button in the Research task pane to display the list of currently activated services.
Notice that the list now includes the Spanish dictionary you just activated.

11. Choose **Research Options** again and remove the **checkmark** from the checkbox to deactivate the Diccionario de la Real Academia Española; click **OK**.

12. Click the **Close** ☒ button in the upper-right corner of the Research task pane.

3.4 Formatting Text

Video Lesson   labyrinthelab.com/videos

FROM THE KEYBOARD
Ctrl+B for bold
Ctrl+U for underline
Ctrl+I for italics

You can format text by changing the font, size, and color, or by applying various enhancements, including bold, italics, and underline. You can change the text formatting before you start typing, or you can select existing text and then make the changes. When you tap Enter, Word continues to use the same formatting until you change it. Two common methods for formatting text include using the Font dialog box or the commands on the Ribbon.

Clearing Text Formatting

TIP

Changes to the font case are not affected by the Clear Formatting command.

Once you have applied formatting, it is very easy to remove. Any selection can be returned to plain text with one click of the Clear Formatting command. You find the Clear Formatting command in the Font group on the Home tab of the Ribbon.

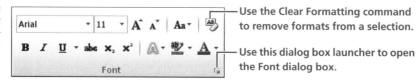

Use the Clear Formatting command to remove formats from a selection.

Use this dialog box launcher to open the Font dialog box.

The following illustration describes the Font dialog box.

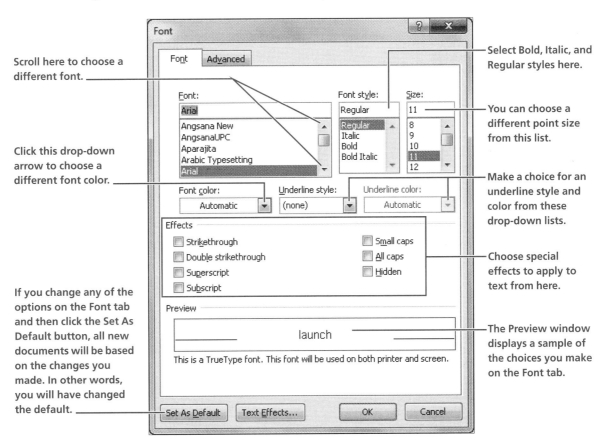

Scroll here to choose a different font.

Click this drop-down arrow to choose a different font color.

If you change any of the options on the Font tab and then click the Set As Default button, all new documents will be based on the changes you made. In other words, you will have changed the default.

Select Bold, Italic, and Regular styles here.

You can choose a different point size from this list.

Make a choice for an underline style and color from these drop-down lists.

Choose special effects to apply to text from here.

The Preview window displays a sample of the choices you make on the Font tab.

3.5 Working with Fonts and Themes

Fonts determine the appearance of the text. There are many fonts installed with Word; some are appropriate for business while others add a more whimsical, personal touch.

A theme is a set of formatting selections including colors, graphic elements, and fonts, all designed to blend well together. The theme-related font choices include one font for body text and one for headings. You will see the actual names of the theme fonts listed in the Font drop-down menu on the Ribbon, but you will see only their generic names, +Body and +Heading, in the Font dialog box. Various themes use different sets of theme fonts.

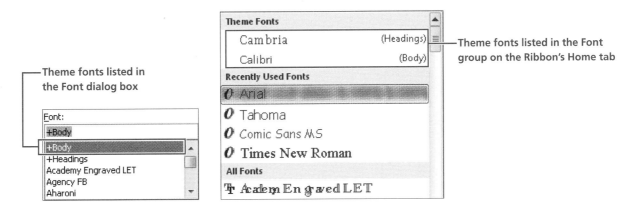

Theme fonts listed in the Font dialog box

Theme fonts listed in the Font group on the Ribbon's Home tab

Changing the Font Case

FROM THE KEYBOARD

[Shift]+[F3] to change font case

Font cases include lowercase, uppercase, sentence case, and capitalize each word. Before beginning to type, if you want the text in uppercase, you can tap the [Caps Lock] key and all text will be capitalized until you tap the key again. Many times though, you may want to change the case after you've already typed the text. In this situation, all you have to do is select the text and apply a different font case. You can change the font case by using the Change Case command in the Font group on the Home tab of the Ribbon or by using [Shift]+[F3] to toggle through the uppercase, lowercase, and capitalize each word commands.

DEVELOP YOUR SKILLS 3.5.1
Format Text

In this exercise, you will use elements from the Font group on the Ribbon, format the text, change the case, and clear formatting.

Format the Press Release Title Lines

1. **Scroll** to the top of the second page.

2. Position the **mouse pointer** in the left margin, and **drag down** to select the first three heading lines.

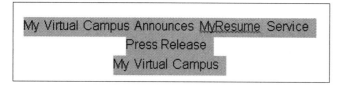

3. Choose **Home→Font→dialog box launcher** 🔲 to display the Font dialog box.

4. Follow these steps to change the font and font size:

Ⓐ Scroll down and choose **Arial** from the Font list.

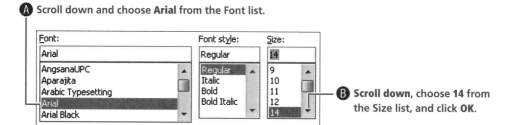

Ⓑ **Scroll down**, choose **14** from the Size list, and click **OK**.

Add Text Enhancements

5. With the three lines still selected, **tap** [Ctrl]+[B] and then **tap** [Ctrl]+[U] to apply bold and underline enhancements to the headings.

6. Click the **Underline** 🔲 button to remove that enhancement.

7. Follow these steps to apply bold formatting to multiple selections at the same time:

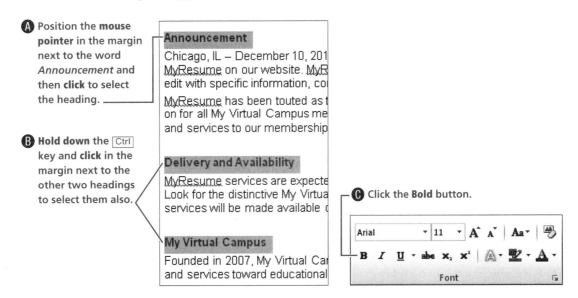

Ⓐ Position the **mouse pointer** in the margin next to the word *Announcement* and then **click** to select the heading.

Ⓑ **Hold down** the `Ctrl` key and **click** in the margin next to the other two headings to select them also.

Ⓒ Click the **Bold** button.

Change the Font Case

8. At the top of the first page, position the **insertion point** at the beginning of the first line, and then **click and drag** over *Memo To*.

9. **Press and hold down** the `Shift` key and **tap** `F3`.
   Notice that the text changed to all uppercase with one tap. If you continued holding down the `Shift` key and tapped `F3` again, it would change to all lowercase, followed by Capitalize Each Word with an additional tap.

10. **Double-click** the word *From*, and then choose **Home→Font→Change Case** ![Aa] from the Ribbon.

11. Choose **UPPERCASE** from the drop-down menu.

12. Using either method above, change the words *Date* and *Subject* to **uppercase**.
    Don't panic here! The reason that the subject text moved to the next half-inch tab stop is because the word Subject *got bigger when you changed it to uppercase—it's an easy fix.*

13. Position the **insertion point** after the colon following SUBJECT and **tap** `Delete` once to remove the extra tab stop.

Clear Formatting from Selected Text

14. Position the **mouse pointer** in the left margin, and then **triple-click** to select the entire document.

15. Choose **Home→Font→Clear Formatting** from the Ribbon.
    Notice that all formatting is removed from the entire document, including all font changes and text alignments, etc. (This does not include changes to the font case.)

16. Click the **Undo** ![undo] button to restore all the formatting.

17. **Save** ![save] your file and leave it **open** for the next exercise.

The Format Painter

Video Lesson   labyrinthelab.com/videos

The Format Painter ![icon] lets you copy text formats from one location to another. This is convenient if you want the same format(s) applied to text in different locations. The Format Painter copies all text formats, including the font, font size, and color. This saves time and helps create consistent formatting throughout a document. The Format Painter is located in the Clipboard group on the Home tab, and it also appears on the Mini toolbar.

QUICK REFERENCE	COPYING TEXT FORMATS WITH THE FORMAT PAINTER
Task	**Procedure**
Copy text formats with the Format Painter	▪ Select the text with the format(s) you wish to copy.
	▪ Click the Format Painter once if you want to copy formats to one other location, and double-click if you want to copy to multiple locations.
	▪ Select the text at the new location(s) that you want to format. If you double-clicked in the previous step, the Format Painter will remain active, allowing you to select text at multiple locations. You can even scroll through the document to reach the desired location(s).
	▪ If you double-clicked, then click the Format Painter button to turn it off.

DEVELOP YOUR SKILLS 3.5.2
Use the Format Painter

In this exercise, you will change the format applied to a heading and use the Format Painter to copy formats from one text block to another.

1. **Scroll** to page 2, if necessary, and **select** the heading *Announcement* just above the first large paragraph of text.

2. When the Mini toolbar appears, follow these steps to apply color to the heading line:

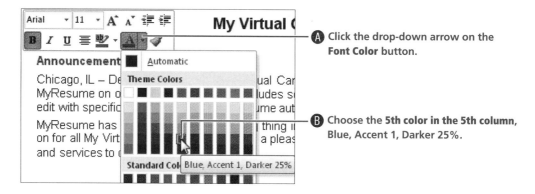

Ⓐ Click the drop-down arrow on the **Font Color** button.

Ⓑ Choose the **5th color in the 5th column**, Blue, Accent 1, Darker 25%.

Notice that the color you selected is in the Theme Colors category. These are the theme colors for Word's default theme.

3. Keep the text selected and the Mini toolbar active, and follow these steps to apply additional formats to the text:

Ⓐ Click the **Italic** button to italicize the text.

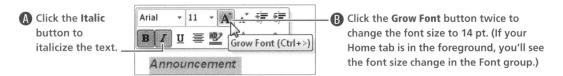

Ⓑ Click the **Grow Font** button twice to change the font size to 14 pt. (If your Home tab is in the foreground, you'll see the font size change in the Font group.)

Copy Formats to One Location

4. Make sure the heading *Announcement* is selected.

5. Click the **Format Painter** 🖌 button on the Mini toolbar.
A paintbrush icon is added to the I-beam mouse pointer once it is positioned over the document.

6. Drag the **mouse pointer** across the *Delivery and Availability* heading, and then **release** the mouse button.
The 14 pt italic blue formats should be copied to the heading. The animated paintbrush icon also vanishes because you clicked the Format Painter button just once in the previous step. If you want to copy formats to multiple locations, you must double-click the Format Painter.

7. Make sure the *Delivery and Availability* heading is still selected.

8. Click the **Format Painter** 🖌 button on the Ribbon and then **select** the last heading, *My Virtual Campus*, to copy the format again.

Copy Formats to More Than One Location

9. **Scroll up** to the top of page 1.

10. **Click** and **drag** over *MEMO TO:* and then click the **Bold** **B** button.
Be sure to include the colon in the MEMO TO: selection so it is formatted also.

11. Make sure *MEMO TO:* is still selected, and then **double-click** the **Format Painter** 🖌 on the Ribbon.

12. **Drag** over *FROM:* to apply the formatting from *MEMO TO:*.

13. **Drag** over *DATE:* and *SUBJECT:* to format these headings also.

14. Choose **Home→Clipboard→Format Painter** 🖌 to turn it off.

15. **Save** 💾 your file and leave it **open** for the next exercise.

3.6 Working with Find and Replace

Video Lesson labyrinthelab.com/videos

FROM THE KEYBOARD
Ctrl+F for Find
Ctrl+H for Replace

Word's Find command lets you search a document for a particular word or phrase. You can also search for text formats, page breaks, and a variety of other items. Find is often the quickest way to locate a phrase, format, or item in a document.

The Find and Replace commands appear in the Editing group at the right end of the Home tab.

Searching with the Navigation Pane

The Find command now displays the new Navigation pane on the left side of the screen. You can search for text or other objects in your document, and the items found will conveniently display in the results area, giving you a quick view of everywhere they appear in the document.

Browse Options

By default, the Find command searches for text; however, with a click of the magnifying glass, you can choose to search for other objects, such as graphics, tables, footnotes, and so forth. At the top of the results window are three tabs that allow you to browse the results by the headings, the pages, or the word(s) you typed in the search box.

When you perform a search, the results are displayed in the navigation pane and are also highlighted in the actual document. You can scroll through the document, locating each instance, or simply click any of the results in the navigation pane to jump to that instance in the document.

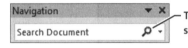

The magnifying glass displays a menu of search options, including objects such as tables or graphics, which you may search for instead of text.

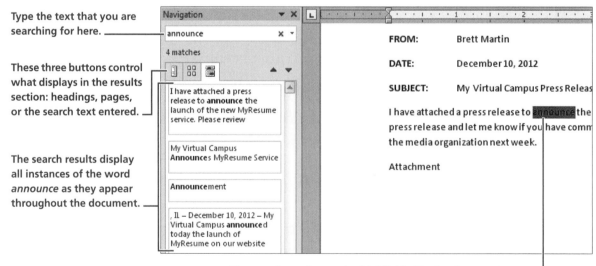

Type the text that you are searching for here.

These three buttons control what displays in the results section: headings, pages, or the search text entered.

The search results display all instances of the word *announce* as they appear throughout the document.

The search results are also highlighted in the document.

Using the Find and Replace Dialog Box

The Replace option in the Editing group on the Home tab displays the Find and Replace dialog box, where you can enter text, an object, or formatting you are searching for and the replacement for the found text, object, or format. You can also use the Go To tab to jump quickly to a specific place such as a page, section, bookmark, and so forth.

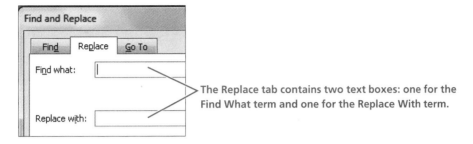

The Replace tab contains two text boxes: one for the Find What term and one for the Replace With term.

If you have already searched for text using the Navigation pane, the text automatically appears in the Find What text box in the Find and Replace dialog box.

Click the Go To button to display a menu of of specific places to jump to.

You type the term you are searching for here.

Click this button if it is labeled More. (The button name toggles between More and Less.) Clicking More displays the bottom half of the dialog box. Clicking Less closes the bottom half.

Notice that the Find and Replace tabs appear within the same dialog box.

Find Next initiates the search.

You can search up or down from the insertion point or through the entire document (All).

The checkboxes let you further qualify your search.

These options allow you to search for formats and other features.

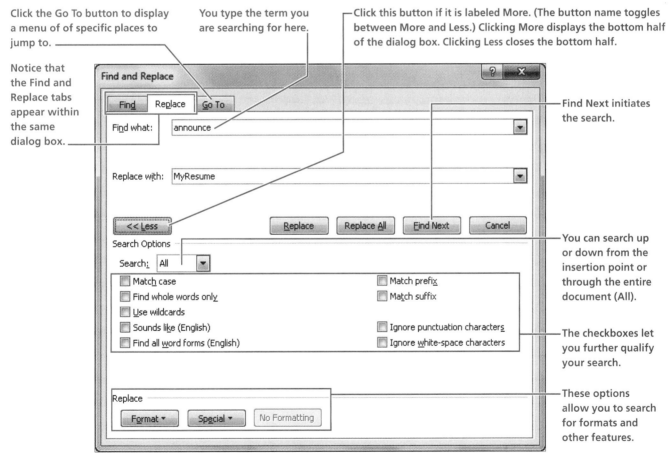

Finding and Replacing Formats

You may want to replace the formats in a document. Perhaps you formatted certain elements with a particular font and now you want to use a different font. Find and Replace finds the formatted elements for you and automatically replaces them.

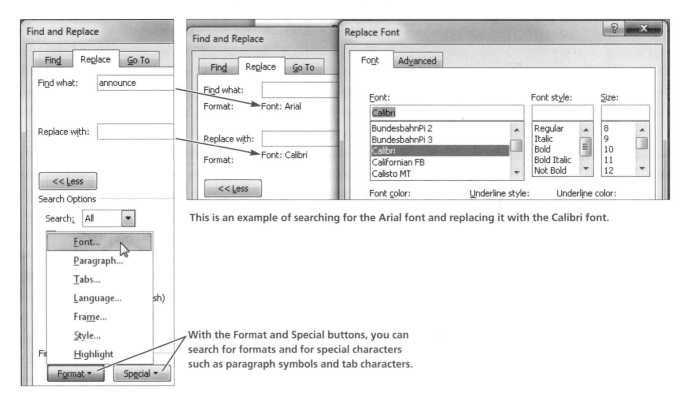

This is an example of searching for the Arial font and replacing it with the Calibri font.

With the Format and Special buttons, you can search for formats and for special characters such as paragraph symbols and tab characters.

DEVELOP YOUR SKILLS 3.6.1

Use Find and Replace

In this exercise, you will search with the Navigation pane, use Find and Replace, and explore some special search options.

Find a Word

1. Position the **insertion point** at the top of page 2, and make sure no text is selected.
2. Choose **Home→Editing→Find** 📖.

3. Follow these steps to find all occurrences of *website*:

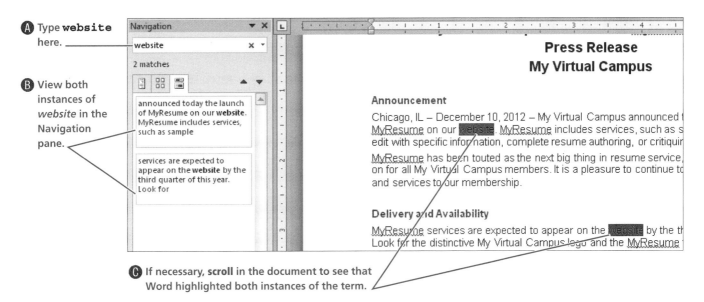

Ⓐ Type **website** here.

Ⓑ View both instances of *website* in the Navigation pane.

Ⓒ If necessary, **scroll** in the document to see that Word highlighted both instances of the term.

4. Scroll to the top of the document, and position the **insertion point** anywhere in the first line of the memo.

Find Another Word

5. Click in the **Navigation pane** search box, delete *website*, and type **Announce** (with a capital A) in its place.
Notice that Word located announce *in the first paragraph of the memo and that* announce *has a lowercase* a, *even though you typed it in uppercase.*

6. Click the second instance in the **Navigation pane** results list and notice that *Announces* is highlighted in the first heading line of the press release.
Notice that Word found Announce, *even though it is part of* Announces. *By default, the search feature is not case sensitive and doesn't recognize the difference between a whole word and part of a word. You will change this, however, in the next few steps.*

Use the Match Case Option

Now you will use the Find Options and Additional Search Commands menu to display the Find and Replace dialog box, and then use Match Case.

7. Follow these steps to display the Find and Replace dialog box:

Ⓐ Click the **Find Options and Additional Search Commands menu ▼** button next to the Search Document box and choose **Advanced Find** from the drop-down menu. Notice that the Navigation pane is no longer the active window since you opened the Find and Replace dialog box.

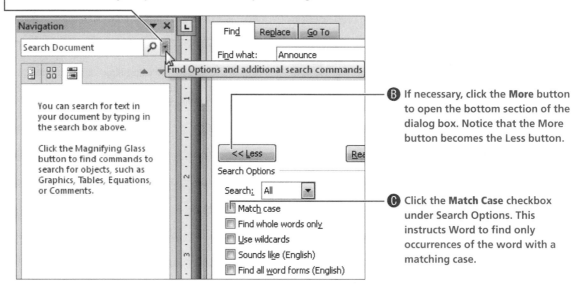

Ⓑ If necessary, click the **More** button to open the bottom section of the dialog box. Notice that the More button becomes the Less button.

Ⓒ Click the **Match Case** checkbox under Search Options. This instructs Word to find only occurrences of the word with a matching case.

8. Click the **Find Next** button, and Word locates the capitalized word *Announcement.*

9. Click **Find Next** again, and Word indicates that the entire document has been searched. *Word skipped over* announced *in lowercase in the next line.*

10. Click **Yes** in the message box.

11. Uncheck the **Match Case** checkbox.

Search for a Whole Word

12. If necessary, **scroll** to the top of the document, and place the **insertion point** anywhere in the first line of the memo.

13. Check the **Find Whole Words Only** checkbox.

14. Click **Find Next** twice, and on the second click Word indicates that the entire document was searched.
    Notice that this time the search did not locate Announces, Announcement, *or* announced.

15. Click **OK** in the message box, and then uncheck the **Find Whole Words Only** checkbox.

16. Delete the word *Announce* in the **Find What** box.

Search for Text Formats

17. Click the **Format** button at the bottom of the dialog box.
    The Format button lets you search for specific fonts, paragraph formats, and other formats.

18. Choose **Font** from the list.

19. Choose **Bold** from the Font Style list, and click **OK**.
    Font: Bold *should appear below the Find What box.*

20. Click the **Find Next** button, and Word selects a word in bold face type.

21. Click the **Less** button to collapse the bottom portion of the dialog box, and then click the **Cancel** button to close the dialog box.

Use Replace

22. Position the **insertion point** at the top of the document, and make sure no text is selected.

23. **Press** Ctrl+H to display the Find and Replace dialog box.
    Notice that the Replace tab is active in the dialog box. The shortcut keystrokes that you use determine which tab displays when the dialog box appears. Make sure the insertion point is in the Find What text box.

24. Click the **More** button to expand the dialog box, and then click the **No Formatting** button at the bottom of the dialog box.
    You need to turn off the Bold formatting option so Find will no longer limit it's results to finding words with Bold formatting.

25. Click the **Less** button to collapse the dialog box.
    The Marketing Department decided to change the name of My Virtual Campus' new feature from MyResume to ResumePlus.

26. Type **MyResume** in the Find What box, and then type **ResumePlus** in the Replace With box.

27. Click the **Find Next** button to locate the first occurrence of *MyResume*.

28. Click the **Replace** button to make the replacement.
    Word moves to the next occurrence of MyResume.

Use Replace All

29. Click the **Replace All** button to make all the changes at once.
    The message box informs you that Word made seven replacements.

 Use Replace All with caution. You should be confident about the replacements Word will make before you use this feature. Using Replace allows you to monitor each replacement.

30. Click **OK** to dismiss the message, and then **close** the Find and Replace dialog box and observe the *ResumePlus* replacements.

31. **Close** the Navigation pane.

32. **Save** 🖫 the file and leave it **open** for the next exercise.

3.7 Navigating in Documents

Video Lesson   labyrinthelab.com/videos

There are more efficient ways to navigate in a document than always using the arrow keys or the scroll bar. Bookmarks and hyperlinks are especially effective in a long document. You can create and use bookmarks to move to new locations within the same document. You may already be familiar with hyperlinks from using the Internet. (Hyperlinks are those blue, underlined links you use to jump from one place to another). Word gives you the ability to do the same thing. A hyperlink in Word uses bookmarks or heading styles to jump to places that are within the same document.

Setting Up Bookmarks

You can assign a bookmark name to selected text or other objects in a document. Once a bookmark is set up, you can easily navigate to it by choosing the desired bookmark name from the Bookmark dialog box or the Go To tab in the Find and Replace dialog box.

You add new bookmarks to the list by typing a name, with no spaces, in the Bookmark Name text box and clicking the Add button.

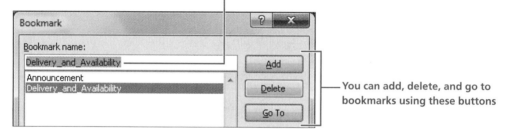

You can add, delete, and go to bookmarks using these buttons

QUICK REFERENCE	USING BOOKMARKS
Task	**Procedure**
Create a bookmark	■ Select the text to use as a bookmark. ■ Choose Insert→Links→Bookmark from the Ribbon. ■ Type the bookmark name without spaces. ■ Click Add.
Jump to a bookmark using the Bookmark dialog box	■ Choose Insert→Links→Bookmark from the Ribbon to open the Bookmark dialog box. ■ Choose a bookmark name from the list and click the Go To button.
Jump to a bookmark using the Find and Replace dialog box	■ Choose Home→Editing→Find from the Ribbon. ■ Click the menu ▼ button next to the Search Document box and choose Go To from the list to open the Find and Replace dialog box. ■ Choose Bookmark from the Go To What box and type or select the Bookmark name, then click the Go To button.

Navigate in Documents

In this exercise, you will create bookmarks and use them to jump to different areas of the document.

Create Bookmarks

1. Before you begin, be sure **page 2** is displayed; then, **select** the word *Delivery* in the second heading.
   Remember, you must first select the text that you want to use as a Bookmark.

2. Choose **Insert→Links→Bookmark** 📝 from the Ribbon to display the Bookmark dialog box.

3. Follow these steps to create a Bookmark:

Ⓐ Type **Delivery_and_Availability** in the Bookmark Name box. Be sure to use the underscores instead of spaces because Bookmark names cannot contain spaces.

Bookmark	? X
Bookmark name:	
Delivery_and_Availability	Add
Delivery_and_Availability	Delete
	Go To

Ⓑ Click the **Add** button.

4. **Scroll**, if necessary, and **select** the Announcement heading.

5. Choose **Insert→Links→Bookmark** 📝 from the Ribbon.

6. Type **Announcement** in the Bookmark Name box, and then click the **Add** button.

Use a Bookmark to Navigate

7. **Press** ⌷Ctrl⌷+⌷Home⌷ to move the insertion point to the beginning of the document.

8. Choose **Insert→Links→Bookmark** 📝 from the Ribbon.

9. Click the Delivery_and_Availability bookmark, and then click the **Go To** button.
   Notice that the Bookmark dialog box remains open just in case you want to jump to somewhere else.

10. Choose the Announcement bookmark and click **Go To**.

11. Click the **Close** ✖ button to close the dialog box.

12. **Press** ⌷Ctrl⌷+⌷Home⌷ to move the insertion point to the beginning of the document.

Using Hyperlinks

Video Lesson   labyrinthelab.com/videos

A hyperlink is a block of text or a graphic that jumps you to another location when clicked, such as to a Bookmark, to another document, or to a web page. Hyperlinks in Word, just like the hyperlinks in web pages, provide the ability to quickly move to another location within the same document or to another document. To use a hyperlink *within* a document, the location you link to must first be set up as a Bookmark or be formatted in a heading style.

There are four primary types of hyperlinks.

- **Hyperlinks to areas within the current document**—This works much like a Bookmark, jumping the reader to another location in the same document.
- **Hyperlinks to other documents or files**—A hyperlink can open another Word document or even another program, such as Excel or PowerPoint.
- **Hyperlinks to web pages**—You can also create a link in a document to jump to a web page by using a URL address for the hyperlink.
- **Hyperlinks to email addresses**—Certain information may require additional clarification from a specific person; thus, you can create a hyperlink to a specific email address. When the hyperlink is clicked, a new message window opens with the email address already in the To: box.

You can remove a hyperlink if it becomes outdated by using the Hyperlink dialog box or by right-clicking the link to display a context menu.

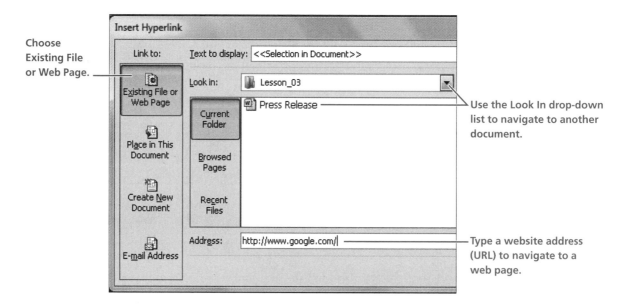

Choose Existing File or Web Page.

Use the Look In drop-down list to navigate to another document.

Type a website address (URL) to navigate to a web page.

DEVELOP YOUR SKILLS 3.7.2

Work with Hyperlinks

In this exercise, you will create a hyperlink and then use it to jump to another document. Then, you will remove a hyperlink.

Create a Hyperlink to Jump to Another Document

1. Select the words *Press Release* in the **Subject** line.

2. Choose **Insert→Links→Hyperlink** 🌐 from the Ribbon.

3. Follow these steps to create a hyperlink to another document:

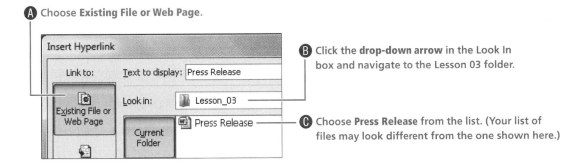

Ⓐ Choose **Existing File or Web Page**.

Ⓑ Click the **drop-down arrow** in the Look In box and navigate to the Lesson 03 folder.

Ⓒ Choose **Press Release** from the list. (Your list of files may look different from the one shown here.)

4. Click **OK** to create the link.
   Notice the words Press Release *change to blue, underlined text.*

Use the Hyperlink

5. **Press** and **hold** ⌑Ctrl⌑ and click the **blue** Press Release link.

6. **Close** the Press Release document but leave the Martin Memo **open**.

Remove a Hyperlink Using the Hyperlink Dialog Box

7. **Click** anywhere in the hyperlink.

8. Choose **Insert→Links→Hyperlink**.

9. Click the **Remove Link** button.

10. **Save** and **close** the Martin Memo document.

3.8 Concepts Review

Concepts Review labyrinthelab.com/word10

To check your knowledge of the key concepts introduced in this lesson, complete the Concepts Review quiz by going to the URL listed above. If your classroom is using Labyrinth eLab, you may complete the Concepts Review quiz from within your eLab course.

Reinforce Your Skills

Practice Formatting

In this exercise, you will practice working with character formats. Use the Font group on the Home Ribbon for steps 3–6 and use the Mini toolbar for steps 7, 8, and 10.

1. **Open** rs-Yard Sale from the Lesson 03 folder.

2. **Tap** Enter a couple times to better align the document on the page.

3. Select the **three heading lines**, and change the font to Arial, bold, and red.

4. **Deselect** the text, and then **select** the first heading line and change it to 18 points.

5. **Select** the second heading line, and make it 14 points.

6. Make the **third heading** line 18 points.

7. Apply **bold** to the date and time in the body.

8. **Select** the body, and change the font to Comic Sans MS or the font of your choice.

9. Place the **insertion point** in front of *Stop* in the body, and **tap** Enter to provide additional space between the heading lines and the body.

10. Change the **heading lines** to a different color of your choice and then change them to uppercase.

11. **Select** the paragraph under the heading lines and note of the number of words in the paragraph versus the entire document.

12. **Save** 🖫 the file and **close** it.

Create a Memorandum

In this exercise, you will create a memorandum. You will also apply character formatting.

1. Follow these guidelines to create the memorandum shown at the end of this exercise:
   - **Position** the line *MEMO TO:* approximately 2 inches down from the top of the page.
   - Apply **bold** to the lead words *MEMO TO:*, *FROM:*, *DATE:*, and *SUBJECT:*.
   - Apply **bold** formatting to the time and date in the body paragraph.
   - Type your **initials** at the bottom of the memo.

2. **Save** 🖫 the memo in the Lesson 03 folder as **rs-Alexander Memo**, and then **close** it.

MEMO TO:	Trevor Alexander
FROM:	Linda Jackson
DATE:	Today's Date
SUBJECT:	Monthly Sales Meeting

Our monthly sales meeting will be held in the conference room at **10:00 a.m.** on **Thursday, January 24.** Please bring your sales forecast for February and be prepared to discuss any important accounts that you wish to. I will give you a presentation on our new products that are scheduled for release in March. I look forward to seeing you then.

xx

REINFORCE YOUR SKILLS 3.3

Use the Spelling Checker and Find and Replace

In this exercise, you will practice using the Find and Replace feature and then spell check the document.

1. **Open** rs-Birds of Prey from the Lesson 03 folder.

2. **Spell check** the document, making the appropriate changes.

3. Use the **Navigation pane** to highlight all instances of *Birds*.

4. Display the **Find and Replace** dialog box from the Navigation pane.

5. **Replace** all occurrences of *Birds of Prey* with *Bird Watcher*.
   Word automatically italicizes the phrase Bird Watcher *because* Birds of Prey *was italicized.*

6. **Save** 🔲 the document, and then **close** it.

REINFORCE YOUR SKILLS 3.4

Use Hyperlinks and Bookmarks

In this exercise, you will create and use hyperlinks and Bookmarks.

1. **Open** rs-Online Neighborhood Sales Notice from the Lesson 03 folder.

2. Create a **hyperlink** on the word *furniture* in the rs-Online Neighborhood Sales Notice document that will jump to the rs-Furniture document in the Lesson 03 folder.

3. Use the **hyperlink** to open the rs-Furniture document.

4. Create a **bookmark** named **Media_Cabinet** for the piece of furniture on the last page.

5. **Scroll** to locate the dresser and create a bookmark for it.

6. Use the **shortcut keystrokes** to return to the beginning of the document.

7. Use the **Bookmark** dialog box to jump down to view the dresser and then view the media cabinet.

8. **Save** and **close** both the rs-Furniture and the rs-Online Neighborhood Sales Notice documents.

Apply Your Skills

Edit a Business Letter

In this exercise, you will get more practice with Find and Replace and the spelling checker feature. You will also make some formatting changes and practice moving text.

1. **Open** as-Ota Letter from the Lesson 03 folder.
   This letter is set up with traditional letter spacing.

2. **Spell check** the document, making any necessary changes.

3. Use **Find and Replace** to replace all occurrences of *bill* with *account*.

4. Use **Find and Replace** to replace all occurrences of *payment* with *check*.

5. Select the entire document, change the font to **Times New Roman**, and change the font size to **12 points**.

6. Use ⌈Enter⌉ to start the date line at approximately the 2-inch position.

7. Replace *Today's Date* with the current date.

8. Move the **address block** from the bottom of the letter to the space between the last body paragraph and the complimentary close *Sincerely.* If necessary, **insert** or **remove** hard returns until there is a double space between the address block and the last body paragraph and between the address block and the complimentary close *Sincerely.*

9. Insert your typist's **initials** below the signature block.

10. **Save** 🖫 the changes, and then **close** the document.

Use the Spelling Checker and Find and Replace

In this exercise, you will practice using the spelling checker and the Find and Replace feature.

1. **Open** as-Collarbone from the Lesson 03 folder.

2. **Spell check** the document. Use your best judgment to determine which replacement words to use for incorrectly spelled words.

3. Use **Find and Replace** to make the following replacements. Write the number of replacements in the third column of the table.

Word	Replace With	Number of Replacements
breaks	fractures	_____
collarbone	clavicle	_____
movement	range-of-motion	_____

4. **Print** the document when you have finished.

5. **Save** 🖫 the changes, and then **close** the document.

Format Characters and Insert Special Characters

In this exercise, you will try out various character formats and insert special characters. Then you will insert and delete a page break.

1. **Open** as-Formatting from the Lesson 03 folder.

2. Follow the instructions in the exercise document to format lines and insert special characters.

3. Change the title at the top of the document to **uppercase** and **underline** it.

4. **Save** 🖫 the document and **close** it.

Critical Thinking & Work-Readiness Skills

In the course of working through the following Microsoft Office-based Critical Thinking exercises, you will also be utilizing various work-readiness skills, some of which are listed next to each exercise. Go to labyrinthelab.com/workreadiness to learn more about the work-readiness skills.

3.1 Use Dates and Symbols

Brett has received positive feedback from early users of MyResume and her press release. She writes a memo to her manager, Rick Smith, reporting some of the feedback. Open ct-Feedback Memo (Lesson 03 folder). Insert a complete and appropriate heading for a memorandum at the top of the document, including To, From, Date, and Subject. Be sure to use the tab stops so the information is nicely formatted and aligned. Add the trademark symbol (™) after *MyResume*. Use Find and Replace to replace all instances of *we have* with **we've**. Save the file to your Lesson 003 folder as **ct-Feedback Final**.

WORK-READINESS SKILLS APPLIED
- Writing
- Serving clients/customers
- Communicating information

3.2 Use Page Breaks and Proofreading Tools

Start with the ct-Feedback Final document you created in the previous exercise and save it to your Lesson 03 folder as **ct-Feedback Points**. Add a final sentence to the first page explaining that specific feedback is on the next page. Insert a page break after the last paragraph and add at least five points of positive feedback from users of MyResume, the online resume builder. Use the spelling and grammar checker throughout the memo, making corrections as necessary. Save your changes.

WORK-READINESS SKILLS APPLIED
- Writing
- Thinking creatively
- Communicating information

3.3 Rewrite and Reformat a Memorandum

Start with the ct-Feedback Points document you created in the previous exercise and save it to your Lesson 03 folder as **ct-Feedback Rewrite**. Use the tools on the Navigation pane to find the first instance of the word *positive* and then replace the word with a synonym you found using the Research task pane. Find and replace the word *potential* with a synonym. Replace at least one other word with a synonym using the Research task pane. Find *MyResume* and turn it into a hyperlink that links to **http://myresume.example.com**. Save your changes.

WORK-READINESS SKILLS APPLIED
- Solving problems
- Selecting technology
- Applying technology to a task

Creating a Simple Report

LEARNING OBJECTIVES

After studying this lesson, you will be able to:

- Create appropriate report formats
- Use paragraph alignment settings
- Use spacing features
- Set custom tab stops
- Format lists
- Apply borders and shading

In this lesson, you will create a simple report. Reports are important documents often used in business and education. You will format your report using various paragraph formatting techniques. Paragraphs are a fundamental part of any Word document. You will learn how to use paragraph alignment techniques, change line spacing, set custom tab stops, and work with Word's indent features. In addition, you will convert text to bulleted and numbered lists and promote and demote the list levels. You will also add interest to the document by applying borders and shading.

Formatting a Research Paper

Kevin Hottel is a business analyst at My Virtual Campus. He has been assigned the task of preparing a report on the importance of computer technology in the 21st

century and how far it has progressed. This report will be a useful tool for management to have as background information. The program manager, John Mathison, asked Kevin to use Word 2010 so he can easily review the report prior to submitting it to his director. After conducting his initial research, Kevin uses paragraph formatting techniques such as borders, bullets, and numbering to prepare an easy-to-read, properly formatted, and professional-looking report.

An Evolution and a Revolution

The Internet is largely responsible for the information explosion we see today. Many people and organizations contributed to its development over many years. The following table shows some high points in the evolution of the Internet.

Year	Event	Responsible Person/Agency
1969	Beginning of the Internet	Advanced Research Projects Agency (ARPANET)
1971	Email invented	ARPANET
1976	Queen Elizabeth sends email	Queen Elizabeth
1990	WWW named	Tim Berners-Lee
1992	"Surfing the Web" coined	Jean Armour Polly
2001	575,000,000 WWW sites	People worldwide

Search Engines

Knowing how to access information on the Internet typically means that you need to be familiar with search engines. Some of the best-known search engines include:

- Google ™
    - o Filed for incorporation in September 1998
      This search engine is tops on many people's list.
- Yahoo!®
    - o Incorporated in March 1995
      Yahoo! is the oldest directory-type search engine and a favorite of many.
- Ask.com™

Popular Programs

1. Word
    a. A Word-processing program used to create letters, reports, books, memorandums, research papers, and so forth.
2. Excel
3. PowerPoint
4. Access

4.1 Formatting Reports

Video Lesson   labyrinthelab.com/videos

There are a variety of acceptable report formats. The following example shows a traditional business report in unbound format. Different report formats can be used for research papers and other types of documents.

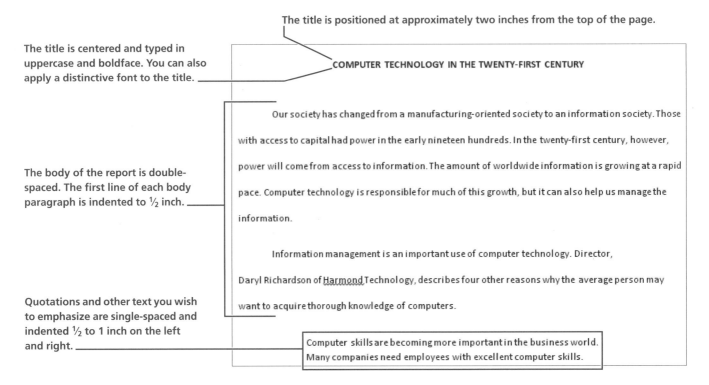

The title is positioned at approximately two inches from the top of the page.

The title is centered and typed in uppercase and boldface. You can also apply a distinctive font to the title.

COMPUTER TECHNOLOGY IN THE TWENTY-FIRST CENTURY

The body of the report is double-spaced. The first line of each body paragraph is indented to ½ inch.

Our society has changed from a manufacturing-oriented society to an information society. Those with access to capital had power in the early nineteen hundreds. In the twenty-first century, however, power will come from access to information. The amount of worldwide information is growing at a rapid pace. Computer technology is responsible for much of this growth, but it can also help us manage the information.

Information management is an important use of computer technology. Director, Daryl Richardson of Harmond Technology, describes four other reasons why the average person may want to acquire thorough knowledge of computers.

Quotations and other text you wish to emphasize are single-spaced and indented ½ to 1 inch on the left and right.

Computer skills are becoming more important in the business world. Many companies need employees with excellent computer skills.

4.2 Using Paragraph Formatting

Paragraph formatting includes paragraph alignment, line spacing, paragraph space settings, and bullets and numbering, to mention a few options.

Selecting paragraphs for formatting purposes is a little different from selecting characters. With character formatting, you select the entire block of text you want to format. In the majority of situations this is necessary. With paragraph formatting, you need only click in the paragraph to *select* it. You can highlight the entire paragraph if you wish, but that is not necessary. On the other hand, if you want to apply formatting to more than one paragraph, you must select at least part of each paragraph.

Paragraph Defined

In Word, a paragraph is created anytime you tap the Enter key. In other words, a paragraph could consist of several lines that end with an Enter or just one line, such as a heading, that ends with an Enter. Tapping Enter to generate a blank line creates a paragraph, even though there is no text in it. What's more, Word stores formats in the paragraph mark.

Paragraph Formatting Compared to Character Formatting

You use character formatting when you wish to format individual words or a selected block of text. Paragraph formatting affects the entire paragraph.

Character formats are available in the Font group of the Home tab on the Ribbon, while paragraph formats appear in the Paragraph group of the Home tab.

Using Paragraph Alignment

Paragraph alignment determines how text aligns between the margins. Left alignment gives the paragraph a straight left margin and a ragged right margin. Center alignment is usually applied to headings. Right alignment generates a straight right and a ragged left margin. Justify provides straight left and right margins. You can use several tools to align paragraphs, including the alignment commands on the Ribbon, the Paragraph dialog box, and the Mini toolbar.

Setting Alignments

The following illustration displays the paragraph alignment commands on the Home tab of the Ribbon. The Center command is also conveniently located on the Mini toolbar.

Examples

The following illustration shows how the different paragraph alignment settings look in Word.

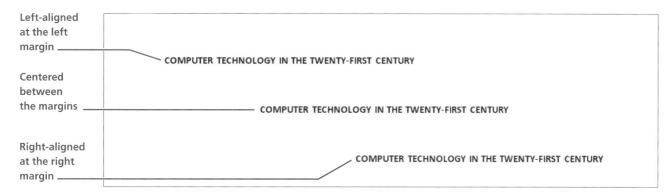

Align Text with the Ribbon and Mini Toolbar

In this exercise, you will practice using the alignment buttons in the Paragraph group of the Home tab and the Center button on the Mini toolbar to align your report heading.

1. **Start** a blank document, and make sure the Word window is **maximized** ▣.

2. If necessary, choose **View→Document Views→Print Layout** ▣ to switch to Print Layout view.

3. If the ruler does not appear on the screen, click the **View Ruler** ▣ button at the top of the scroll bar.

4. **Tap** Enter enough times to position the insertion point approximately 2 inches from the top of the page.

Type the Heading

5. Turn on Caps Lock and choose **Home→Font→Bold** **B** from the Ribbon.

6. **Type** the report title, **COMPUTER TECHNOLOGY IN THE TWENTY-FIRST CENTURY.**

7. **Turn off** Bold and Caps Lock, and then **tap** Enter twice.

8. Position the **insertion point** in the report heading.

Align the Heading

9. Choose **Home→Paragraph→Center** ▤ from the Ribbon.

10. Choose **Home→Paragraph→Align Text Right** ▤ from the Ribbon.

11. Choose **Home→Paragraph→Align Text Left** ▤ from the Ribbon.

12. **Right-click** on the heading to display the Mini toolbar.

13. Click the **Center** ▤ button on the toolbar to center the heading.

14. **Save** the file in the Lesson 04 folder as **Computer Report,** leave the file **open,** and continue with the next topic.

Setting Line Spacing

Video Lesson labyrinthelab.com/videos

FROM THE KEYBOARD

Ctrl+1 for single spacing

Ctrl+5 for 1.5 spacing

Ctrl+2 for double spacing

The Line Spacing ▤ button in the Paragraph group of the Home tab lets you set line spacing for one or more paragraphs. Word 2010's default line spacing is 1.15. You apply line spacing by selecting the desired paragraph(s) and then choosing the desired line spacing from the Line Spacing drop-down list, or by using one of the keyboard shortcuts.

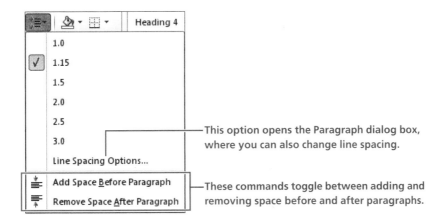

This option opens the Paragraph dialog box, where you can also change line spacing.

These commands toggle between adding and removing space before and after paragraphs.

Inserting a Nonbreaking Space

FROM THE KEYBOARD

Ctrl + Shift + Spacebar to insert a nonbreaking space

Most of the time, you take advantage of one of Microsoft Word's oldest and dearest features, Word Wrap, which allows you to keep typing by wrapping the text at the end of each line until you press Enter at the end of the paragraph. However, you may want to keep two or more words together on the same line. For example, you should keep a first and last name or a complete date on the same line. For these special cases, you can insert a nonbreaking space to control the word(s) that wrap to the next line. You can use the Symbols group on the Insert tab to insert the special character that creates a nonbreaking space; however, tapping Ctrl + Shift + Spacebar is a much quicker method.

Adding Hyphenation

Typically, when you create a document in Word, you let Word Wrap do its thing; that is, it adds all of the text it can on a line until it comes to a word that won't fit. Since that word is too long, it is moved down to the next line. Sometimes this can cause your right margin to become very jagged. To have a more evenly spaced document, you can use the Hyphenation feature found in the Page Setup group on the Page Layout tab of the Ribbon. You have two basic options when activating the Hyphenation menu: automatic or manual hyphenation.

- **Automatic**—The entire document is hyphenated automatically and since you did not enter any manual hyphens, as you edit or revise the document, automatic hyphenation continues as you type.

- **Manual**—You can also set the Hyphenation feature to manual, which goes through the document searching for instances where hyphenation is required. You then get to choose whether or not to hyphenate each word.

DEVELOP YOUR SKILLS 4.2.2
Set Line Spacing

In this exercise, you will begin by changing to double-spacing. Then you will return to single-spacing for several paragraphs in the document.

1. If necessary, choose **Home→Paragraph→Show/Hide ¶** to display formatting characters.

2. Position the **insertion point** on the second paragraph symbol below the title.

3. Choose **Home→Paragraph→Line and Paragraph Spacing** ⬍≣ from the Ribbon, and click **2.0** for double-spacing.

4. **Tap** the ⎡Tab⎤ key once to create a $^1/_2$-inch indent at the start of the paragraph.

5. Now **type** the following paragraph, but only **tap** ⎡Enter⎤ once after the last line in the paragraph, since double-spacing is in effect.
The lines will be double-spaced as you type them.

> Our society has changed from a manufacturing-oriented society to an information society. Those with access to capital had power in the early nineteen hundreds. In the twenty-first century, however, power will come from access to information. The amount of worldwide information is growing at a rapid pace. **Computer** technology is responsible for much of this growth, but it can also help us manage the information.

6. Make sure you **tap** ⎡Enter⎤ after the last line. **Tap** ⎡Tab⎤ once, and type the following lines.
Notice that the Word Wrap feature has split the director's first and last name on two lines.

> Information management is an important use of computer technology. Director, Daryl
> Richardson

7. Position the **insertion point** in front of *Richardson* and **tap** ⎡Backspace⎤.
Notice that now Daryl *and* Richardson *are on the same line but do not have a space separating the first and last name. If you tap the spacebar, it will put* Daryl *back on the previous line.*

Insert a Nonbreaking Space

Now you will insert a special character that will move Daryl *to the next line so his name won't be split on two lines.*

8. Make sure the **flashing insertion point** is between the *l* and the *R* between Daryl's first and last name.

9. **Press** and **hold** ⎡Ctrl⎤+⎡Shift⎤ and **tap** the ⎡Spacebar⎤.
Notice that the director's complete name is now on the next line with a space separating the first and last name.

10. **Tap** ⎡End⎤, **tap** the ⎡Spacebar⎤, and finish **typing** the rest of the paragraph.
The completed paragraph should look like the following illustration.

> Information management is an important use of computer technology. Director,
> Daryl Richardson of Harmond Technology, describes four other reasons why the average person may want to acquire thorough knowledge of computers.

11. **Tap** ⎡Enter⎤ to complete the paragraph, and then change the line spacing to **1.15**.

12. Now **type** the following paragraphs, **tapping** ⌷Enter⌷ between paragraphs. You don't need to **tap** ⌷Enter⌷ twice because of the default additional spacing after paragraphs. Do not tab at the beginning of these paragraphs.

Computer skills are becoming more important in the business world. Many companies need employees with excellent computer skills.

Computer skills can often simplify one's personal life. Computers can be used to entertain, to manage finances, and to provide stimulating learning exercises for children.

Using computers can provide a sense of accomplishment. Many people suffer from "computerphobia." Learning to use computers often creates a feeling of connection with the information age.

The Internet and other information resources provide access to a global database of information.

13. **Save** your document, and continue with the next topic.

4.3 Indenting Text

Video Lesson   labyrinthelab.com/videos

Indenting offsets text from the margins. You can set indents by using the Paragraph dialog box, dragging the indent markers on the horizontal ruler, or using buttons on the Ribbon.

Adjusting Indents

The Increase Indent 🔲 and Decrease Indent 🔲 commands on the Home tab of the Ribbon let you adjust the left indent only. These buttons increase or decrease the left indent to the nearest tab stop. Word's default tab stops are set every half inch, so the left indent changes half an inch each time you click either command.

This paragraph is indented with a first-line indent. It offsets only the first line of a paragraph from the left margin; this produces the same result as tapping the ⌷Tab⌷ key to start a paragraph.

This paragraph is indented with a left indent, which offsets all lines in a paragraph from the left margin.

Computer skills are becoming more important in the business world. Many companies need employees with excellent computer skills.

Computer skills can often simplify one's personal life. Computers can be used to entertain, to manage finances, and to provide stimulating learning exercises for children.

Using computers can provide a sense of accomplishment. Many people suffer from "computerphobia." Learning to use computers often creates a feeling of connection with the information age.

The Internet and other information resources provide access to a global database of information.

This is a hanging indent, which leaves the first line of the paragraph at the left margin but indents all other lines.

This paragraph is indented from both the left and right margins. A right indent offsets all lines from the right margin. This is most often used to offset a special notation or quote in the middle of the page and is usually accompanied by a left indent.

Experiment with Left Indents

In this exercise, you will use the Increase Indent and Decrease Indent buttons to indent the last four paragraphs.

Indent One Paragraph

1. **Click** in one of the four paragraphs you just typed.

2. Choose **Home→Paragraph→Increase Indent** 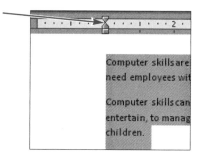 from the Ribbon.
   The paragraph should be indented $1/2$ inch on the left.

3. Choose **Home→Paragraph→Decrease Indent** from the Ribbon to remove the indent.

Indent Several Paragraphs

4. Position the **mouse pointer** in the left margin next to the first paragraph beginning with *Computer skills*, then **drag down** to select it and the next paragraph.

5. Choose **Home→Paragraph→Increase Indent** twice to create a 1-inch left indent on each of the selected paragraphs.
   Notice that the indent markers on the ruler change position when you use the Increase Indent button. You will learn more about that in the next topic.

6. Now click **Decrease Indent** twice to remove the indents.
   Again, notice the indent markers on the ruler.

7. **Save** the file. You will continue to work with indents in the next exercise.

Setting Custom Indents on the Ruler

Video Lesson   labyrinthelab.com/videos

You can set indents by dragging the indent markers on the horizontal ruler. The following illustration shows the ruler and the indent markers.

Indent Markers

The indent markers at the left edge of the ruler are made up of two pieces: a top piece and a bottom piece (see the following illustration). You can drag these two pieces independently of each other. The top piece controls the first line of the paragraph when you drag it to the left or right. The bottom piece is a little trickier. It is made up of two sections, but the sections do not come apart. The bottom piece functions differently, depending on whether you place the tip of the mouse in the triangle or the rectangle. Dragging the bottom triangle affects the *rest* of the paragraph (everything but the first line). Dragging the rectangle affects *both triangles,* positioning the first line and all subsequent lines of the paragraph simultaneously.

You use the indent marker at the right end of the ruler to indent the paragraph from the right.

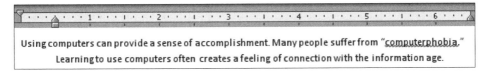

Indents the first line of a paragraph.

Dragging the top triangle to the right makes a hanging indent (see note below).

Indents all lines of a paragraph from the left.

Indents all lines of the paragraph from the right.

Hanging indents are not often used, so many people are not familiar with the term. The following illustration shows an example of a hanging indent, where the first line is *outdented* and the remaining lines of the paragraph are *indented*.

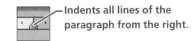

Using computers can provide a sense of accomplishment. Many people suffer from "computerphobia." Learning to use computers often creates a feeling of connection with the information age.

DEVELOP YOUR SKILLS 4.3.2
Use the Indent Marker to Indent Paragraphs

In this exercise, you will practice using the indent markers on the horizontal ruler.

Set Left and Right Indents

1. **Select** all four paragraphs at the bottom of the document.

2. Follow these steps to adjust the left and right indents:

Ⓐ Position the **mouse pointer** on the Left Indent marker (the bottom rectangle).

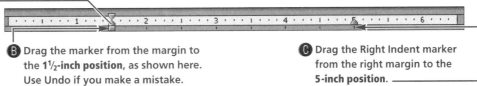

Ⓑ Drag the marker from the margin to the 1½-**inch position**, as shown here. Use Undo if you make a mistake.

Ⓒ Drag the Right Indent marker from the right margin to the **5-inch position.**

Experiment with the Indent Markers

In this section of the exercise, you will focus on the first single-spaced, indented paragraph and experiment further with the indent markers.

3. Make sure all four paragraphs are still **selected**.

4. Position the **mouse pointer** on the First Line Indent marker (the top triangle), and **drag** it to the right to the 2-inch mark on the ruler.
This indents the first line of each paragraph. Remember, the top and bottom pieces can move independently of each other.

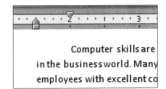

5. Position the **mouse pointer** on the Left Indent marker (rectangle), and **drag** it to the right to the 2-inch mark on the ruler.

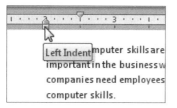

This causes the top and bottom pieces to move simultaneously. Whether they are lined up on top of each other or not, the top and bottom indent markers move simultaneously when you drag the rectangle.

6. Place the **mouse pointer** on the top triangle, and **drag** it left to the 2-inch mark. *The two pieces should be on top of each other.*

7. Feel free to experiment with the indent markers.

8. When you finish, place both pieces of the left markers at the **1-inch** position and the Right Indent marker at **5½ inches**, as shown in the following illustration.

9. **Save** the file, and leave it **open** for the next exercise.

4.4 Using Custom Tab Stops

Video Lesson   labyrinthelab.com/videos

Default tab stops are set every ½ inch, so the insertion point moves ½ inch whenever you tap the Tab key. You can change the tab stops if you want the insertion point to move a smaller or larger distance when you tap Tab or when you want to use a special tab, such as a center tab or a right-align tab. Custom tab stops are also useful for creating leader lines. For example, the dots you see in a table of contents leading to the page numbers are an example of leader lines on a right-aligned tab.

Never use the spacebar to line up columns of text. Even if it looks right on the screen, it will not print correctly.

Setting Custom Tab Stops with the Ruler

Word provides four types of custom tab stops: left, right, center, and decimal. You can set all four types using the horizontal ruler. You set tabs by choosing the desired tab type from the Tabs box at the left end of the ruler. Then you click at the desired location on the ruler to set the tab. The tab is set for the selected paragraph and for each line thereafter as long as you keep tapping the Enter key. You can move a custom tab stop by dragging it to a different location on the ruler.

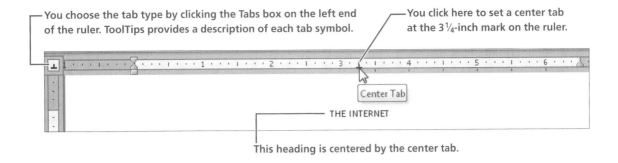

You choose the tab type by clicking the Tabs box on the left end of the ruler. ToolTips provides a description of each tab symbol.

You click here to set a center tab at the 3¼-inch mark on the ruler.

Center Tab

THE INTERNET

This heading is centered by the center tab.

DEVELOP YOUR SKILLS 4.4.1
Set Tabs Using the Ruler

In this exercise, you will use custom tabs to set up text in a columnar format.

1. Move the **insertion point** to the bottom of the page and, if necessary, **tap** Enter to generate a blank line at the bottom of the document.

2. **Tap** Ctrl + Enter to insert a page break.

3. Set the left and right indent markers at the **margins**, as shown here.

4. Choose **Home→Paragraph→Show/Hide** ¶ from the Ribbon to turn on formatting marks.

5. Select the paragraph symbol at the top of **page 2**.
Remember, paragraph symbols carry formatting, so you must select the symbol to format it.

6. Choose **Home→Paragraph→Line and Paragraph Spacing** ↕≡ from the Ribbon, and choose **Remove Space After Paragraph** from the menu.

7. Choose **Home→Paragraph→Show/Hide** ¶ from the Ribbon to turn off formatting marks.

Set Custom Tabs
You will set a center tab for the heading on page 2. Although you may be more likely to use the Center align button for this purpose, this will be good practice in setting tabs.

8. Follow these steps to set and use a center tab:

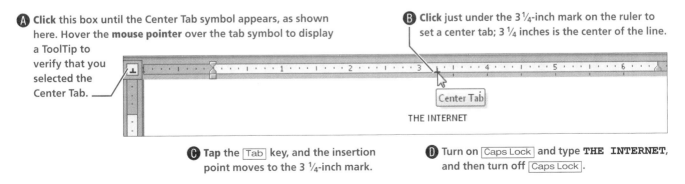

Ⓐ **Click** this box until the Center Tab symbol appears, as shown here. Hover the **mouse pointer** over the tab symbol to display a ToolTip to verify that you selected the Center Tab.

Ⓑ **Click** just under the 3¼-inch mark on the ruler to set a center tab; 3¼ inches is the center of the line.

Center Tab

THE INTERNET

Ⓒ Tap the Tab key, and the insertion point moves to the 3¼-inch mark.

Ⓓ Turn on Caps Lock and type **THE INTERNET**, and then turn off Caps Lock.

9. **Tap** Enter twice.

Notice that the center tab is still in effect. Custom tab stops are paragraph formats, so they are carried to new paragraphs when you tap Enter. *(Remember, Word stores formatting in paragraph marks.) Keep in mind that you could leave the custom tab stops in the new paragraph, even though you will not use them. However, you will remove them to keep your document from becoming cluttered.*

10. **Save** your file, and leave it **open** for the next exercise.

Working with the Tabs Dialog Box

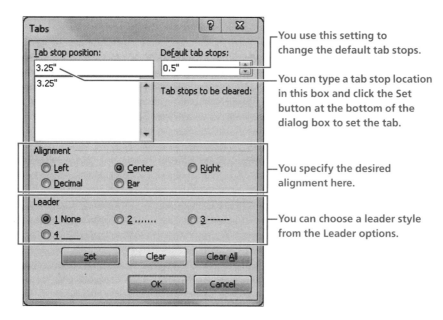

Video Lesson   labyrinthelab.com/videos

You can also set custom tab stops in the Tabs dialog box. You access the dialog box by clicking the dialog box launcher in the Paragraph group of the Home tab and then clicking the Tabs button. In the dialog box, you can specify precise positions for custom tabs, clear custom tab stops, and set leader tabs.

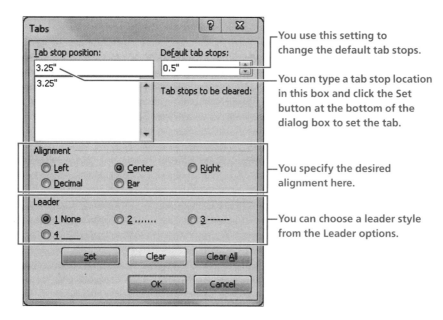

You use this setting to change the default tab stops.

You can type a tab stop location in this box and click the Set button at the bottom of the dialog box to set the tab.

You specify the desired alignment here.

You can choose a leader style from the Leader options.

DEVELOP YOUR SKILLS 4.4.2
Use the Tabs Dialog Box

In this exercise, you will use the Tabs dialog box to clear tabs and to set custom tabs.

Clear Tab Stops

1. Make sure the **insertion point** is in the second line below the heading line.

2. Click the **dialog box launcher** ⬛ in the bottom-right corner of the Paragraph group on the Home tab.

3. Follow these steps to clear the custom tab stop:

Ⓐ Click the **Tabs** button in the Paragraph dialog box to open the Tabs dialog box.

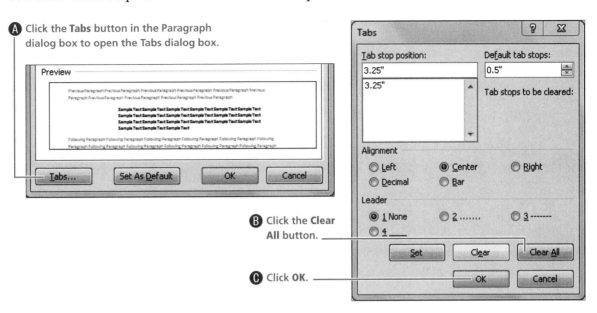

Ⓑ Click the **Clear All** button.

Ⓒ Click **OK**.

Next, you will type a heading and introductory paragraph for your tabular table.

4. Type **An Evolution and a Revolution**, and then **tap** ⎡Enter⎤.

5. Type the following paragraph:

> The Internet is largely responsible for the information explosion we see today. Many people and organizations contributed to its development over many years. The following table shows some high points in the evolution of the Internet.

Now you will set the tabs for a to display text in columns.

Set Custom Tabs with the Dialog Box

6. Tap ⎡Enter⎤ twice, and then click the **dialog box launcher** 🗗 in the Paragraph group on the Home tab.

7. Click the **Tabs** button in the bottom-left corner to display the Tabs dialog box.

8. Follow these steps to set three left tabs:

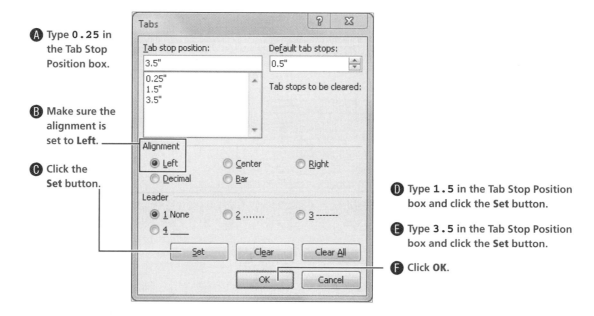

A Type **0.25** in the Tab Stop Position box.

B Make sure the alignment is set to **Left**.

C Click the **Set** button.

D Type **1.5** in the Tab Stop Position box and click the **Set** button.

E Type **3.5** in the Tab Stop Position box and click the **Set** button.

F Click **OK**.

Notice the tab symbols on the ruler. Now you will type the table column headings.

9. Tap the ⌷Tab⌷ key and type **Year**.

10. Tap ⌷Tab⌷ and type **Event**.

11. Tap ⌷Tab⌷ and type **Responsible Person/Agency**, and then **tap** ⌷Enter⌷.
Notice that the insertion point moves to the left margin of the next line. Even though the tab stops are carried to the new paragraph, you must tap ⌷Tab⌷ to actually use the tab stop.

12. Tap ⌷Tab⌷ to align the insertion point below *Year*.

13. Continue **typing** and **tabbing** to create the text as shown in the following illustration. Remember to **tap** ⌷Tab⌷ at the beginning of each line.

Year	Event	Responsible Person/Agency
1969	Beginning of the Internet	Advanced Research Projects Agency (ARPANET)
1971	Email invented	ARPANET
1976	Queen Elizabeth sends email	Queen Elizabeth
1990	WWW named	Tim Berners-Lee
1992	"Surfing the Web" coined	Jean Armour Polly
2001	575,000,000 WWW sites	People worldwide

14. When you finish, apply **Bold** **B** to the column headings.

15. Save your file, but leave it **open** for the next exercise.

Modifying Tab Stops with the Ruler

Video Lesson   labyrinthelab.com/videos

To adjust a tab setting on the ruler, you select the lines containing the tab stops you want to change, and then simply drag the tab symbol to the new location. To delete a tab stop, you just drag the tab symbol off the ruler.

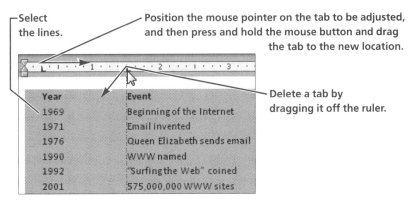

If you accidently drag a tab stop off the ruler while trying to move it, just click Undo.

DEVELOP YOUR SKILLS 4.4.3
Modify and Delete Tab Stops from the Ruler

In this exercise, you will use the ruler to modify the tab stop for the second column. Then you will delete tab stops.

Reposition a Tab Stop

1. Position the **mouse pointer** in the margin next to the column heading line, then **drag down** to select all the lines through the 2001 line.
   Be careful to only select the lines containing the tab stops you want to change. Do not select any blank lines above or below the selection. Now you are ready to adjust the tab position.

2. Position the **mouse pointer** on the tab stop at the 1½-inch position, **press** and **hold** the mouse button, and **drag** to the left to the 1¼-inch position, and then **release** the mouse button. (Use Undo if you make a mistake.)

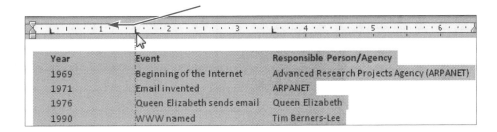

   The entire column moves to the left.

3. Position the **insertion point** at the end of the last line, and **tap** Enter twice.

Delete the Tab Stops

4. Make sure your **insertion point** is on the second blank line.

5. Position the **mouse pointer** over the tab symbol at the $^1/_4$-inch position, and then **press** and **hold** the mouse button and drag straight down into the document.

6. **Release** the mouse button, and the tab is no longer on the ruler.

7. **Repeat** that process to remove the remaining tabs at $1^1/_4$ inches and $3^1/_2$ inches.

8. **Save** the file but leave it **open**, as you will use it in the next exercise.

4.5 Using Bulleted and Numbered Lists

Video Lesson   labyrinthelab.com/videos

Using bulleted or numbered lists is an effective way to make items of interest stand out in a document. You can turn them on before you begin typing, or apply the desired command after you type the list. For example, rather than listing items in a paragraph separated by commas, entering them as a bulleted or numbered list makes them much simpler to read. Numbered lists are automatically renumbered if you insert or delete an item. A good example of when to use a numbered list is when the sequence is important, as in a series of steps. The items in a bulleted list have no sequence.

Converting Text to Lists

You can type all of your text first in regular paragraph format and then add bullets or numbers later simply by selecting the text and clicking the desired command. Remember, text is considered a paragraph each time you press the Enter key; thus, when you type a list of names, for instance, each line is considered a paragraph. When you create a bulleted or numbered list, Word applies a hanging indent, where the line with the bullet or number remains at the left and the text is indented under the first line of text.

This is a hanging indent, which leaves the first line with the bullet at the left margin (in this case) but indents all other lines.

- Computer skills are becoming more important in the business world. Many companies need employees with excellent computer skills.
- Computer skills can often simplify one's personal life.
- Computers can be used to entertain, to manage finances, and to provide stimulating learning exercises for children.

In the preceding figure, notice that the remaining lines in the first bulleted paragraph are aligned under the word *Computer* rather than being aligned back out to the left, under the bullet. Note that all bulleted lines do not have to start at the margin; they can be indented to the right. However, a hanging indent is still created for the subsequent lines.

Promoting and Demoting List Items

Demoting a list item increases the indent level by shifting text to the right. Similarly, promoting decreases the indent level and moves the text (with its bullet or number) back to the left. When you demote items in a numbered list, it creates an outline effect, indicating the level of importance of the items in the list. In addition to using the indent buttons on the Ribbon, you can use the [Tab] key to demote an item and [Shift]+[Tab] to promote a list item. When you tap [Enter], Word maintains the same list level as the previous paragraph.

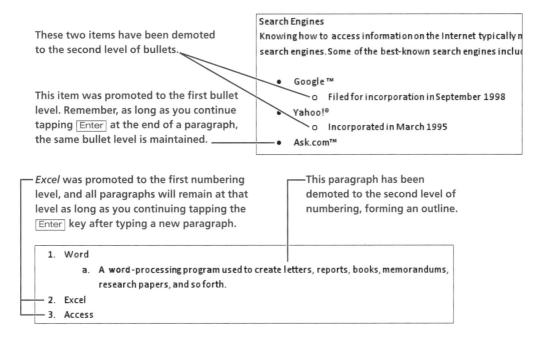

These two items have been demoted to the second level of bullets.

This item was promoted to the first bullet level. Remember, as long as you continue tapping [Enter] at the end of a paragraph, the same bullet level is maintained.

Search Engines
Knowing how to access information on the Internet typically n
search engines. Some of the best-known search engines inclu

- Google ™
  - o   Filed for incorporation in September 1998
- Yahoo!®
  - o   Incorporated in March 1995
- Ask.com™

Excel was promoted to the first numbering level, and all paragraphs will remain at that level as long as you continuing tapping the [Enter] key after typing a new paragraph.

This paragraph has been demoted to the second level of numbering, forming an outline.

1. Word
   a. A word-processing program used to create letters, reports, books, memorandums, research papers, and so forth.
2. Excel
3. Access

Turning Off Bullets and Numbering

When you are finished with the list, you should tap [Enter] to position the insertion point on the next line. You then turn off the bullets or numbering command using the buttons on the Ribbon or by simply tapping [Enter] once more.

QUICK REFERENCE	WORKING WITH LISTS
Task	**Procedure**
Convert text to a bulleted or numbered list	▪ Select the text to be formatted as a list. ▪ Choose Home→Paragraph→Bullets [☰]. *or* ▪ Choose Home→Paragraph→Numbering [☰].

WORKING WITH LISTS (continued)

Task	Procedure
Turn off bullets and numbering	■ Tap ⟦Enter⟧ at the end of the last list item. ■ Choose the Bullets ⊞ or Numbering ⊞ button. *or* ■ Tap ⟦Enter⟧ one more time.
Demote items in a list	■ Select the items to demote one level to the right. ■ Choose Home→Paragraph→Increase Indent ⊞. *or* ■ Tap the ⟦Tab⟧ key.
Promote items in a list	■ Select the items to promote one level to the left. ■ Choose Home→Paragraph→Decrease Indent ⊞. *or* ■ Hold down ⟦Shift⟧ and tap ⟦Tab⟧.

DEVELOP YOUR SKILLS 4.5.1

Work with Bullets and Numbering

In this exercise, you will convert a list to bullets, promote and demote levels, and create a numbered list.

Create a Bulleted List

1. Make sure the **insertion point** is two lines below the tabbed text table. Then **type** the following heading and introductory paragraph:

> Search Engines
> Knowing how to access information on the Internet typically means that you need to be familiar with search engines. Some of the best-known search engines include:

2. **Tap** ⟦Enter⟧ twice at the end of the paragraph.

3. Type **Google(tm)** as the first search engine and then **tap** ⟦Enter⟧ to position the insertion point on the next line.
   Notice that after you type the (tm), *Word automatically replaces it with the* ™ *symbol.*

4. Finish typing the list as shown, **tapping** ⟦Enter⟧ after each item.

> Google ™
> Filed for incorporation in September 1998
> Yahoo!®
> Incorporated in March 1995

Convert Text to a Bulleted List

5. Position the **mouse pointer** in the margin area to the left of the *Google*™ line and **drag down** to select all four lines in the list.

6. Choose **Home→Paragraph→Bullets** :≡ from the Ribbon.
   Notice all four lines have bullets and are on the same level; you will fix that in just a minute by demoting certain lines.

Demote a List Item

7. **Select** the second bulleted line, *Filed for incorporation in September 1998.*

8. **Tap** Tab to demote the line one level under the Google™ heading.

9. **Select** the last line and then click the **Increase Indent button** ⋛ on the Ribbon.

10. Position the **insertion point** at the end of the last line and **tap** Enter.
    Notice that the new line is still at the indented level. In this case, it needs to be promoted one level so you can type a new search engine.

Promote a List Item

11. **Hold down** Shift and then **tap** Tab to promote the new line.
    The new line moves one level to the left so it matches the other search engines.

12. Type **Ask.com(tm)** and **tap** Enter.

13. **Tap** Enter three times to turn off the bullets and leave an extra blank line after the list.

Create a Numbered List

14. Type **Popular Programs** and **tap** Enter.

15. Choose **Home→Paragraph→Numbering** ≟≡ from the Ribbon.

16. **Type** the list, demoting and promoting as shown, and then **tap** Enter twice after the final list entry.

> 1. Word
>   a. A word-processing program used to create letters, reports, books, memorandums, research papers, and so forth.
> 2. Excel
> 3. Access

17. Position the **insertion point** after *Excel* and **tap** Enter.
    Notice that there is now a new line three and Access *became line four.*

18. Type **PowerPoint** as the new line three.

19. **Save** the document and leave it **open** for the next exercise.

Using the Bullets and Numbering Libraries

Video Lesson labyrinthelab.com/videos

The menu buttons  on the Bullets and Numbering buttons provide access to bullets and numbering libraries, where you can choose a style for your bulleted or numbered list or define new formats.

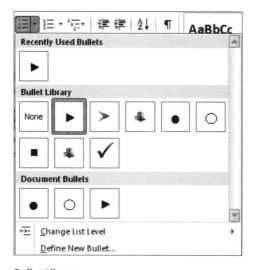

The bullets and numbering libraries shown in the following illustrations display the available built-in styles.

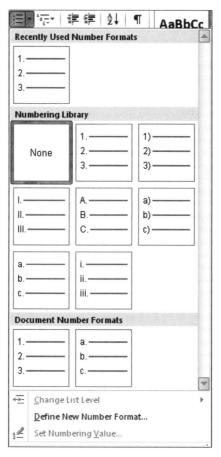

Bullet Library

Numbering Library

Change the Bullet Style

In this exercise, you will choose a different bullet style from the bullets gallery.

1. Select the **first bulleted line**.

2. While **holding down** the Ctrl key, **select** the *Yahoo!* and *Ask.com* lines, as shown here.

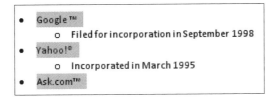

- Google ™
  - o   Filed for incorporation in September 1998
- Yahoo!®
  - o   Incorporated in March 1995
- Ask.com™

3. Click the drop-down arrow on the **Bullets** button and choose the circle bullet. *The position of the circle bullet in the library may vary.*

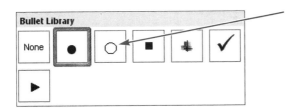

4. **Save** your file, and leave it **open** for the next exercise.

Customizing Bullet and Number Styles

Video Lesson   labyrinthelab.com/videos

Bullet styles can be customized by defining a symbol, picture, font, or alignment. You can also customize the number style, font, and alignment. You can define a new bullet or number format by clicking the drop-down arrow on the Bullets or Numbering button and choosing Define New Bullet or Define New Number Format from the list.

You can choose from a variety of symbols, pictures, and fonts.

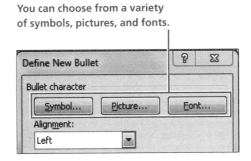

You can select a number style from this list.

You can choose from a variety of fonts to customize your numbering style.

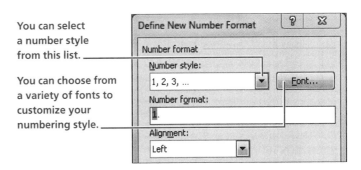

Restart or Continue Numbering

Many documents have more than one numbered list. Sometimes you may want the numbering to continue sequentially from one list to the next. For example, if one list ends with the number 4 you may want the next list to begin with the number 5. If you type a paragraph after the first list, when you begin the next list in your document, Word assumes you want to restart numbering at 1. If you want to continue numbering from the previous list, Word provides an AutoCorrect smart tag when you start additional numbered lists in a document. You can click the AutoCorrect Options smart tag and choose Continue Numbering.

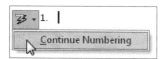

Experiment with Custom Bullets

In this exercise, you will work with the Define New Bullet dialog box.

1. **Click** anywhere in one of the three bulleted search engine lines.

2. Choose **Home→Paragraph→ Bullets** ▤ ▾ **menu ▾** to display the Bullets library, and then choose **Define New Bullet** from the bottom of the menu.

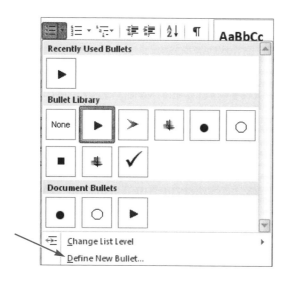

3. Follow these steps to define a picture as a new bullet:

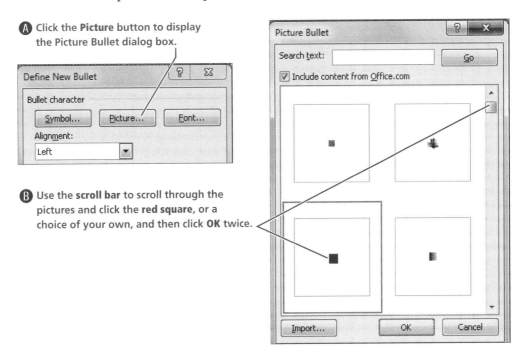

Ⓐ Click the **Picture** button to display the Picture Bullet dialog box.

Ⓑ Use the **scroll bar** to scroll through the pictures and click the **red square**, or a choice of your own, and then click **OK** twice.

Notice that all the Level 1 bullets have changed to the new custom bullet.

4. Choose **Home→Paragraph→Bullets** menu ▼ to display the Bullet Library.

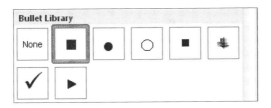

Notice that the new custom bullet now appears in the library, although its location and the number of bullets in the library on your screen may differ from the preceding illustration.

5. Click anywhere in the document to **close** the library.

If you wish to remove a bullet from the library, right-click it and choose Remove from the context menu.

6. Click the *Google* line and then click the **Bullets** menu button one more time and choose the original black bullet.

7. **Save** the document and leave it **open** for the next exercise.

4.6 Setting Line Breaks

Video Lesson labyrinthelab.com/videos

When working with bullets and numbering, tapping [Enter] generates a new bullet or number. What if you want to type something relative to a bulleted or numbered item on the next line(s) without generating a new bullet or number? A manual *line break* starts a new line (without inserting a paragraph mark) and continues the text on the new line. The new line is part of the same paragraph as the preceding line. Line breaks are inserted with the [Shift]+[Enter] keystroke combination.

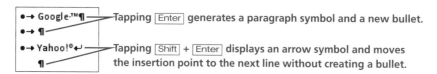

Tapping [Enter] generates a paragraph symbol and a new bullet.

Tapping [Shift] + [Enter] displays an arrow symbol and moves the insertion point to the next line without creating a bullet.

DEVELOP YOUR SKILLS 4.6.1
Insert Line Breaks in a List

In this exercise, you will use line breaks to add descriptive information about the items in the search engine list.

1. Place the **insertion point** after *1998* in your bulleted list.

2. **Tap** [Shift]+[Enter] to generate a line break rather than a paragraph break.

3. If necessary, click the **Show/Hide** [¶] button to see the line break, which appears as a small arrow at the end of the line. Then click **Show/Hide** again to turn off formatting marks.

4. **Type** the following: **This search engine is tops on many people's list.** *If you were to tap* [Enter] *at this point, Word would generate a new bullet because you started a new paragraph.*

5. **Click** at the end of *1995* in the line under *Yahoo!* and **tap** [Shift]+[Enter] to generate a line break.

6. **Type** the following: **Yahoo! is the oldest directory-type search engine and a favorite of many.**

7. **Save** your file and leave it **open**, as you will use it in the next exercise.

Using the Paragraph Space Settings

Video Lesson labyrinthelab.com/videos

The following illustration of the Paragraph group on the Page Layout tab shows the default 10-point after-paragraph spacing. You can use the spinner controls on the Before and After Spacing buttons to adjust the amount of space. You can also use the spacing controls in the Paragraph dialog box in the same way.

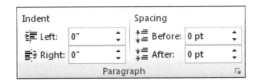

Paragraph spacing controls on the Ribbon in the Paragraph group on the Page Layout tab.

Paragraph spacing controls in the Paragraph dialog box.

Paragraph Spacing Defined

A point (pt) is just 1/72nd of an inch. This fine unit of measure, common in printing, facilitates great precision. Word uses points for type size and other settings, such as paragraph spacing.

72 points = 1 inch   36 points = $^1/_2$ inch   24 points = $^1/_3$ inch

DEVELOP YOUR SKILLS 4.6.2

Set Paragraph Spacing

In this exercise, you will add 4 points of paragraph spacing between the headings and the introductory paragraphs on page 2.

1. **Select** the heading *An Evolution and a Revolution* near the top of page 2.

2. Click the **Page Layout** tab to display its Paragraph group.

3. In the Spacing area, click in the **After** box and type **4**, and then **tap** Enter.
   Notice the additional space following the heading.

The spinner controls in the Spacing area use 6 point increments for spacing. If you wish to use a different measurement, you must enter it manually.

4. **Select** the *Search Engines* heading, and then type **4** in the After box and **tap** Enter.

5. Use the same technique to add **4 points** of extra space after the heading *Popular Programs*. *You could have used the Format Painter to copy the formatting from the first heading, but this was a good opportunity to practice with the spacing controls.*

6. **Save** the file, and leave it **open** for the next exercise.

4.7 Using Borders and Shading

Video Lesson labyrinthelab.com/videos

You can apply borders and shading to selected text, paragraphs, and objects, such as tables or drawing shapes. Page borders are also available to outline an entire page. In this lesson, you will concentrate on applying borders to paragraphs. Paragraph borders are the lines applied to the top, bottom, left, and right edges of a selected paragraph, and they extend from the left to right margin. Thus, if you only want a border surrounding a specific amount of text, you must select only that text and be careful not to select the paragraph mark. You can choose the style, color, and thickness of borders, and you can also select various shading patterns and colors.

The Borders Button

Clicking the Borders ⊞▾ menu ▾ button in the Paragraph group of the Home tab on the Ribbon displays a menu of border options. The Borders and Shading command at the bottom of the menu opens the Borders and Shading dialog box.

The borders button has a memory. It displays the last choice you made from the menu on the button face. That way you can apply the same type of border several times in a row without opening the menu. The button name changes accordingly.

Example

The border button that appears when you first start Word is named Bottom Border; it looks like this: ⊞

If you apply an outside border, as an example, the button is named Outside Border; it looks like this: ⊞

The Shading Button

The ⬛ Shading ▾ button located in the Paragraph group of the Home tab provides a quick way to apply shading. Shading is the background color of the selected area. For example, if you select text, it is the background color behind the text. However, if you apply a paragraph border, it is the background color inside the border that extends from margin to margin.

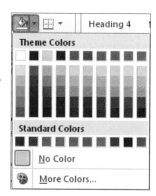

The Borders and Shading Dialog Box

Video Lesson   labyrinthelab.com/videos

Choose Borders and Shading from the Borders ⊞ ▾ menu ▾ on the Ribbon to display the dialog box. The following illustrations show the features available in the Borders tab and the Shading tab of the dialog box.

Remove borders or specify a particular type of border here.

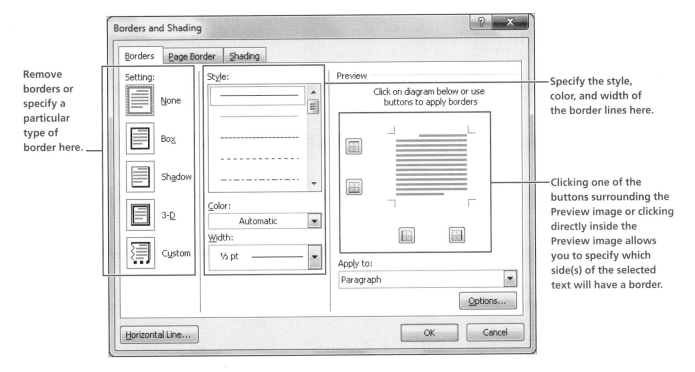

Specify the style, color, and width of the border lines here.

Clicking one of the buttons surrounding the Preview image or clicking directly inside the Preview image allows you to specify which side(s) of the selected text will have a border.

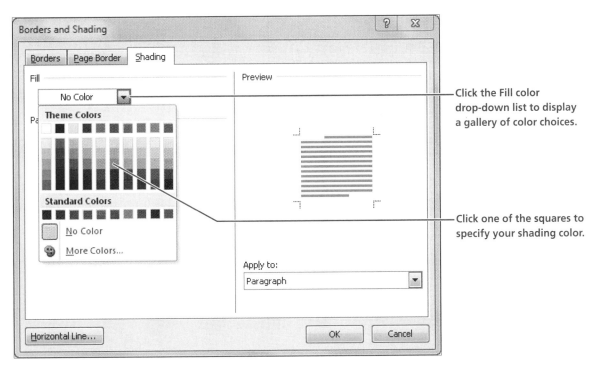

Click the Fill color drop-down list to display a gallery of color choices.

Click one of the squares to specify your shading color.

Apply a Border and Shading to Headings

In this exercise, you will apply borders and shading to the paragraph headings on page 2, using the Borders and Shading dialog box.

1. **Click** anywhere in the line *An Evolution and a Revolution*.

2. Choose **Home→Paragraph→Borders** 🔲 **menu ▼** from the Ribbon, and then choose the **Borders and Shading** command at the bottom of the gallery to display the dialog box.

3. Make sure the **Borders** tab at the top of the dialog box is in the foreground.

4. Follow these steps to apply a border to the first heading:

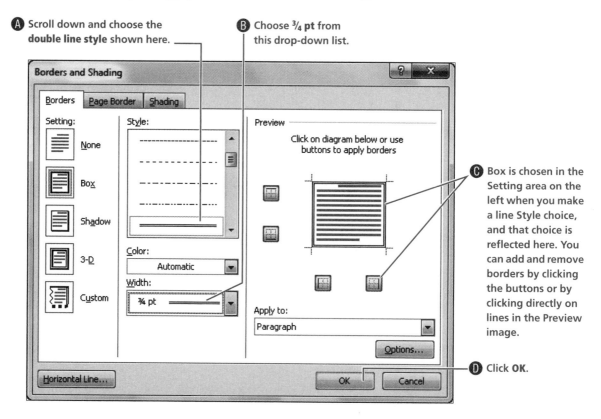

Ⓐ Scroll down and choose the **double line style** shown here.

Ⓑ Choose ¾ pt from this drop-down list.

Ⓒ Box is chosen in the Setting area on the left when you make a line Style choice, and that choice is reflected here. You can add and remove borders by clicking the buttons or by clicking directly on lines in the Preview image.

Ⓓ Click **OK**.

Notice that the border extends between the margins. Paragraph borders fill the space between the margins, unless the paragraph(s) are indented.

5. Choose **Home→Paragraph→Borders** 🔲 **menu ▼** from the Ribbon; choose the **Borders and Shading** command at the bottom of the gallery.

6. Click the **Shading** tab, and then click the **Fill** color drop-down list.

7. Choose **Tan, Background 2, Darker 10%** from the list, as shown in the following illustration, and then click **OK**.

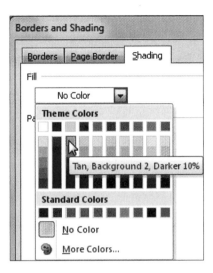

Use the Format Painter to Copy the Heading Formats

8. Make sure your **insertion point** is still in the heading *An Evolution and a Revolution*.

9. Double-click the **Format Painter** 🖌. Remember, double-clicking keeps the Format Painter turned on.

10. **Select** the *Search Engines* heading, and then **select** the *Popular Programs* heading to format the headings.

11. Click **Format Painter** 🖌 again to turn it off.

12. **Save** the file, and leave it **open** for the next exercise.

4.8 Inserting Page Numbers

Video Lesson   labyrinthelab.com/videos

You can insert page numbers at various positions on a page. Page numbers are inserted at the top or the bottom of the page and may be aligned at the left margin, centered, or right-aligned.

A page numbering gallery offers a variety of page numbering designs. Choose Insert→Header & Footer→Page Number from the Ribbon to display a menu of positions for your page numbers. Choose a position, and then click the desired style to insert page numbers in your document.

Insert Page Numbers

In this exercise, you will insert page numbers in your report.

1. Choose **Insert→Header & Footer→Page Number** [#] from the Ribbon.

2. Follow these steps to insert page numbering:

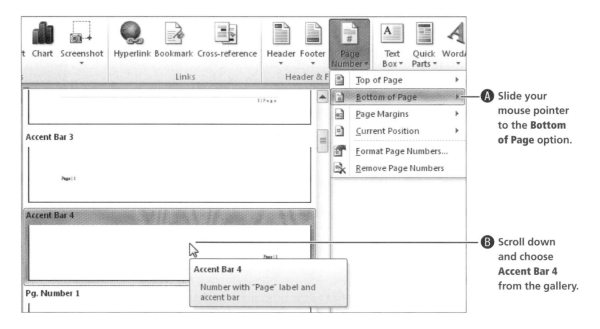

3. **Double-click** the body of the document to close the footer area.

4. **Scroll** through the document and **observe** the page numbering.
   The numbering appears grayed out, but it will print like normal text.

5. **Save** your report and **close** it.

4.9 Concepts Review

Concepts Review   labyrinthelab.com/word10

To check your knowledge of the key concepts introduced in this lesson, complete the Concepts Review quiz by going to the URL listed above. If your classroom is using Labyrinth eLab, you may complete the Concepts Review quiz from within your eLab course.

Reinforce Your Skills

Create a Policies and Procedures Document

In this exercise, you will use multiple lists to create a policies and procedures page. You will also use Word's demote, promote, and indent commands to organize the lists.

Add Numbering

1. **Open** the rs-Outdoor Adventures file from the Lesson 04 folder.

2. **Select** the three lines of text under the *Medical* heading.

3. Choose **Home→Paragraph→Numbering** ⬚ from the Ribbon to convert the text to a numbered list.

4. Convert the lines of text under the *Refunds* and *Cancellations* headings to a **numbered list**.

Add Bullets

5. **Select** the first heading, **hold down** the ⬚Ctrl⬚ key, and **select** the remaining two headings.

6. Choose **Home→Paragraph→Bullets** ⬚ from the Ribbon.

7. **Tap** ⬚Enter⬚ after the *Inclement weather conditions* line, then **tap** ⬚Tab⬚.

8. Type **Over 100 degrees** and **tap** ⬚Enter⬚.

9. Type **Below 60 degrees**, **tap** ⬚Enter⬚, and **tap** ⬚Shift⬚+⬚Tab⬚.

10. Finish **typing** the document as shown at the end of the exercise on the following page.

Define a Custom Bullet

11. **Select** the three bulleted headings.

12. Choose **Home→Paragraph→Bullets** ⬚▾ menu ▾ from the Ribbon.

13. Open the **Define New Bullet** dialog box and choose a new picture of your choice for the selected bullets.

Work with Indents

14. **Select** the numbered lists below each heading.

15. Chose **Home→Paragraph→Increase Indent** ⊞ once to line up the numbered lists under their heading.

16. **Select** the body of the document, excluding the title and subtitle.

17. Chose **Home→Paragraph→Increase Indent** ⊞ to reposition the body, as shown below.

18. **Save** the file and then **close** it.

OUTDOOR ADVENTURES

Policies and Procedures

■ Medical

   1. All guests must have medical insurance
   2. All guests must sign an injury waiver
   3. All guests agree to pay out-of-pocket medical expenses

■ Refunds

   1. A full refund will be given for cancellations with 60-day notice
   2. A 50% refund will be given for cancellations with 30-day notice
   3. No refund for cancellations with less than 30-day notice

■ Cancellations

   1. Inclement weather conditions
      a. Over 100 degrees
      b. Below 60 degrees
   2. Poor water flow
      a. Water level drops to 20 feet
   3. Insufficient number of guests
      a. Ten-guest minimum

REINFORCE YOUR SKILLS 4.2

Create a Tabular Phone List

In this exercise, you will use tabs, paragraph alignment, and line breaks to create the phone list shown at the end of this exercise.

1. **Press** Ctrl + N to open a blank document.

2. If necessary, display the **ruler** at the top of the screen.

3. Because you know this list will be rather short, **tap** Enter four times to position the insertion point approximately $2\frac{1}{2}$ inches from the top of the page.

4. Type **My Virtual Campus**.

5. **Tap** Enter twice.

6. Make sure the **left tab** symbol displays here. If not, **click** the box until it appears.

7. Use the **Ruler** to set a left tab at $1/2$ inch.

8. Now change the tab type to a **right-align tab**; click the **box** until the symbol shown here appears.

9. Set a **right-align** tab at the **6-inch** mark on the ruler.

Add a Leader to a Tab

10. Click the **dialog box launcher** ⌷ in the bottom-right corner of the Paragraph group on the Home tab.

11. When the Paragraph dialog box appears, click the **Tabs** button in the bottom-left corner.

12. Follow these steps to set a tab leader line:

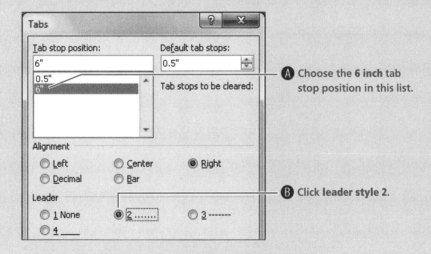

13. Click **OK**.

14. **Tap** the Tab key, and type **Advertising Department**.

15. **Tap** Tab to position the insertion point at the right-align tab, type **312-555-1234**, and then **tap** Enter.

16. Following the illustration at the end of the exercise, continue **typing** the list to the end of the *Accounting* line. Remember to **tap** Tab at the beginning of each new line.

17. Notice the line break symbol at the end of the Accounting line.

18. Insert a line break by **tapping** Shift + Enter.

19. Type **Billing** on the next line.
Because Word does not consider a line break to be a paragraph, it does not take on the additional after-paragraph spacing that Word 2010 adds by default.

20. Tap [Enter], and then **tap** [Tab] and type the last line of the list.

21. **Select** and **center** the title and change the font size to **18 points**.

22. **Save** the document in the Lesson 04 folder as **rs-Phone Directory**, and then **close** it.

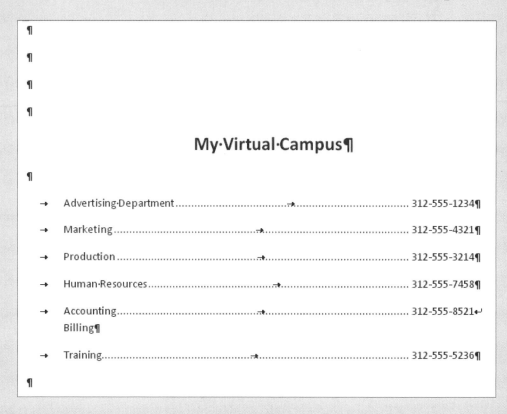

Create a Report with Indents and Bullets

In this exercise, you will open a document from your exercise files. You will format the document until it matches the document on the following page.

1. **Open** rs-Electric Cars from the Lesson 04 folder.

2. Look at the document at the end of this exercise on the following page, and notice the title shown at the top of the document. Insert the **title** at the top margin (1 inch from the top of the page).

3. **Tap** [Enter] twice after the title.

4. **Format** the title with a 14-point bold font, and center-align the title.

5. Select the first **three body paragraphs**, and apply **double-spacing** to them. Turning on the Show/Hide feature will help you distinguish among the first three paragraphs.

6. Adjust the **first line indent** of the first three body paragraphs to $1/2$ inch.

7. Position the **insertion point** at the end of the first line and **remove the space** after the word *United*.

8. Insert a **nonbreaking space** between the words *United* and *States*.

9. **Select** the next six paragraphs, starting with *Affordability*.

10. Apply the **bullet style** shown to the six paragraphs.

11. Use ⌈Tab⌉ to demote the bulleted paragraphs below each heading.

12. **Indent** the last paragraph 1 inch on both the left and right, as shown.
    Your completed document should match the example at the end of this exercise.

13. **Save** the changes to the document, and **close** it.

ELECTRIC CARS

Many people are not aware that electric cars have been used almost ninety years in the United States. In fact, before the introduction of the gasoline automobile, approximately 50,000 electric cars soared down American streets. Presently, electric cars are gaining attention as an effective means of improving our air quality, reducing pollution, and reducing the need to import oil into the United States.

Often referred to as "zero-emission vehicles," electric cars have the distinct advantage of releasing little or no pollution, thereby reducing the amount of carbon monoxide in our air. Electric cars are also quieter than gasoline-fueled cars, and the batteries that power these cars have the potential to be recharged through renewable sources such as wind and solar power.

Steven Lough of Eco-Motion Electric Cars in Seattle, WA, highlights a few of the many benefits of electric cars. A summary of his points follows:

- Affordability
  - Electric cars are affordable.
- Efficiency
  - Electric cars are three times more efficient per dollar than gasoline-fueled cars. They improve air quality, limit pollution, and lessen U.S. dependence on imported oil.
- Batteries
  - Electric cars will improve over time. Already new batteries—including metal-nickel-hydride batteries and lithium batteries—are being researched. In the coming years these batteries will be available, doubling and tripling the per charge rate of these automobiles.

Lough adds a powerful statement, saying that:

> There are alternatives [to gasoline automobiles and the pollution and expense associated with them]...There are carpooling, public transportation, bicycles, telecommunications, and yes, electric cars.

Apply Your Skills

Use Borders, Shading, and Lists in a Flyer

In this exercise, you will create a flyer that Lakeville Community Hospital will distribute through their Health Education Department. You will add borders and shading to headings, use paragraph alignment, and create bulleted lists. When you complete the exercise, your document should look like the figure at the end of this exercise.

1. **Open** the file as-Osteoporosis from the Lesson 04 folder.

2. **Select** the title and subtitle, and **format** them with bold, center alignment, and 16-point font.

3. **Format** the next line, *What is Osteoporosis?*, with bold and 12-point font.

4. **Indent** the next paragraph 1 inch from both the left and the right margins.

Add a Border

5. Select the next line, and click the drop-down arrow on the **Borders** command in the Paragraph group of the Home tab to apply an **Outside Border**. Word will apply the border line style that was last used during the current Word session.
   Remember that the appearance of the Borders button reflects the last choice made from the menu during the current Word session.

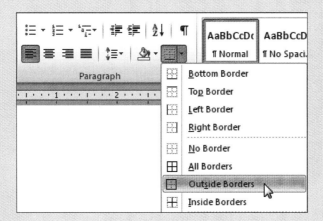

Add Shading

Make sure the line is still selected.

6. Click the drop-down arrow on the **Shading** 🪣 command next to the Borders command.

7. Choose the **shading** you prefer from the gallery.

8. Choose **Home→Clipboard→Format Painter** 🖌 to copy the formatting to the heading *What Can You Do to Help Prevent Falls?*

Add Bullets to Lists

9. **Select** *Get enough calcium* through *Know whether you are at risk*.

10. Apply **bullets** to the list.

11. Apply **bullets** to the seven lines at the end of the document.

12. **Select** both bulleted lists and apply a **different bullet style** of your choice.

13. **Save** the file and **close** it.

Lakeville Community Hospital
Partners in Prevention

What is Osteoporosis?

Osteoporosis is a disorder that causes your bones to become increasingly porous, brittle, and subject to fracture. Women are four times more likely to suffer from osteoporosis than men. However, there are steps you can take to reduce the risk of bone loss and fracture.

WHAT CAN YOU DO TO PREVENT OSTEOPOROSIS?

- Get enough calcium
- Take vitamin D
- Make activity and exercise part of each day
- Stop smoking
- Cut down on caffeine, salt, and alcohol intake
- Know whether you are at risk

WHAT CAN YOU DO TO HELP PREVENT FALLS?

- Have your vision checked
- Stay active to help maintain balance, strength, and coordination
- Wear low-heeled shoes with non-slip soles
- Tie your shoe laces
- Replace slippers that are stretched out of shape and are too loose
- Eliminate all tripping hazards in your home
- Install grab bars and handrails

Use Line Spacing, Numbering, and Indenting

In this exercise, you will format a document with variable line spacing, a numbered list, and indents.

1. **Open** the as-Success document from the Lesson 04 folder.

2. Follow these guidelines to format the document as shown at the end of this exercise:
   - Run the **spelling checker**, making changes as necessary.
   - **Tap** [Enter] enough times to place the insertion point at approximately the 1-inch mark in the vertical ruler.
   - Change the **title** to uppercase, bold, with a 16-point font.
   - Center the **title**; **tap** [Enter] twice after the title.
   - Use **single-spacing** and **double-spacing** as necessary to format the document as shown.
   - Set the **First Line** indent of the two body paragraphs to ¹/₂ inch, as shown.
   - Replace the **space** after the name *Ralph* with a nonbreaking space.
   - Adjust the **indents** of the numbered paragraphs and the quotation, as shown.

3. **Save** the document and then **close** it.

SUCCESS

The quest for success is a driving force in the lives of many Americans. This force drives the

business world and often results in huge personal fortunes. However, success can come in many forms,

some of which are listed below.

    1.   Many people in America view success monetarily.

    2.   Our society also views public figures such as movie stars, athletes, and other celebrities

        as being successful.

    3.   Educational achievement, such as earning an advanced degree, is often perceived as

        successful.

It is easy to see that success means many things to many people. The well-known poet,

Ralph Waldo Emerson, provides this elegant definition of success:

> To laugh often and much; to win the respect of intelligent people and the affection of
> children; to earn the appreciation of honest critics and endure the betrayal of false
> friends; to appreciate beauty; to find the best in others; to leave the world a bit better,
> whether by a healthy child, a garden patch, or a redeemed social condition; to know
> even one life has breathed easier because you have lived. This is to have succeeded.

Critical Thinking & Work-Readiness Skills

In the course of working through the following Microsoft Office-based Critical Thinking exercises, you will also be utilizing various work-readiness skills, some of which are listed next to each exercise. Go to labyrinthelab.com/ workreadiness to learn more about the work-readiness skills.

4.1 Format a Report

Brett is creating a short report on the benefits of new wireless technology—and how it will affect My Virtual Campus users. Open ct-Wireless (Lesson 04 folder) and save a copy of it as **ct-Wireless Report**. Add a centered heading with the text **The New Wireless**. Set the line spacing of all paragraphs to 1.5. Experiment with different paragraph alignments and choose the alignment you feel is the most appropriate. Save your changes. If working in a group, discuss why you believe your choice of alignment is the best choice. If working alone, type your answer in a Word document named **ct-Questions** saved to your Lesson 04 folder.

WORK-READINESS SKILLS APPLIED

- Thinking creatively
- Writing
- Serving clients/ customers

4.2 Add Custom Bullets and Shading

Brett wants to add some custom bullets and shading to the report to make it more readable and interesting to others. Start with the ct-Wireless Report you created in the previous exercise and save a copy of it to your Lesson 04 folder as **ct-Wireless Tabs**. Add a bulleted list at the bottom with at least three benefits of the new wireless technology (be creative with these) and change the default bullet to a checkmark. Add a border and background shading to the heading. Save your changes.

WORK-READINESS SKILLS APPLIED

- Writing
- Thinking creatively
- Serving clients/ customers

4.3 Finalize Report Formatting

Brett is ready to put the finishing touches on the report before distributing it. Start with the ct-Wireless Tabs you created in the previous exercise and save a copy of it to your Lesson 04 folder as **ct-Wireless Final**. Experiment with various paragraph/heading alignments and line spacing. Change the bullets to something other than checkmarks and change the left indent of the bulleted items. Feel free to change the font style and size, too! Use these options to format the report so it is easy to read and maintains a professional feel, yet looks distinctly different from the original ct-Wireless Tabs version. Save your changes.

WORK-READINESS SKILLS APPLIED

- Thinking creatively
- Making decisions
- Selecting technology

Working with Tables and Forms

LEARNING OBJECTIVES

After studying this lesson, you will be able to:

- Insert a table in a document
- Modify, sort, and format tables
- Perform calculations in tables
- Apply built-in table styles
- Create, modify, and use forms
- Set editing restrictions in forms

A table is one of Word's most useful tools for organizing and formatting text and numbers. Tables are flexible and easy to use. Word provides a variety of features that let you set up, modify, and format tables. In this lesson, you will merge and split table cells, sort rows, quickly apply table styles, and perform calculations within tables. You will also create a form by inserting form fields and learn how to protect the form so only the user can enter data.

Student Resources   labyrinthelab.com/word10

Creating Student Tables and a Form

Bethanie Harmon is an administrative assistant for the Product Development Team at My Virtual Campus. The team is always looking for new ideas to enhance the websites. Bethanie has a few ideas of her own that may be useful for students: a survey to help them determine how much money they might need for personal expenses, a list of expenses with totals, and a simple layout for viewing their class schedules. She decides to create tables and a form to present her ideas at the next product development meeting.

Although it has been awhile since Bethanie has created a table, she is up to the task. She knows Word has powerful table and form tools, and she knows it won't take long to brush up her skills and get the tables and the form created.

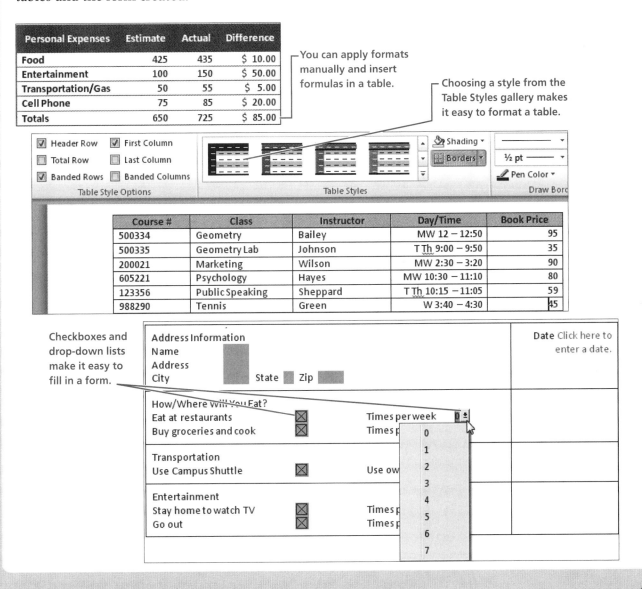

5.1 Introducing Tables

Video Lesson labyrinthelab.com/videos

Tables are a convenient way to lay out data in a columnar format without relying on tab stops, which can sometimes cause a little frustration. You can perform simple calculations in a Word table, although you cannot include the complex calculations that you can perform in Excel. In addition to using a table for a simple columnar layout with calculations, tables may be used to create a resumé or a company letterhead with a logo, or to present information in a format similar to the Quick Reference tables found in this book.

Viewing Gridlines

Certain tables, such as resumes, are most appropriate without applying borders around the cells. However, when creating the tables, it may be easier to maneuver around if there are lines. This is where gridlines come into play. Gridlines appear on the screen as blue dotted lines around each cell in the table, but they do not print. You view table gridlines using the View Gridlines command in the Table group on the Layout tab under Table Tools.

If borders have been applied to a table, the gridlines will not be visible; thus, you must remove all borders first to have the gridlines displayed.

Navigating in a Table

FROM THE KEYBOARD

Tab to move to the next cell

Shift + Tab to move to the previous cell

Tables are made up of cells (rectangles) displayed in a grid with horizontal rows and vertical columns. You can select one or more cells, rows, or columns and then insert, edit, or format them just like you do other text in a document. Tapping Tab when the insertion point is in the last cell of a table automatically adds a new row to the bottom.

DEVELOP YOUR SKILLS 5.1.1
Navigate and Enter Data

In this exercise, you will practice navigating in a table and enter data in it.

Navigate in a Table

1. **Open** the Student Tables document in the Lesson 05 folder.

2. Click in the first cell of the **Expense** table to position the insertion point.

3. **Tap** Tab two times to move to the end of the first row.

4. **Tap** Tab again to move to the beginning of the second row.

5. **Tap** Shift + Tab twice to move backwards, one cell at a time.

6. Position the **insertion point** in the last cell in the last row and **tap** Tab.
   A new row is added to the end of the table.

7. Click **Undo** to remove the new row.

Enter Data

8. Position the **insertion point** in the first cell and then **type** the information shown in the following table. Remember to use [Tab] to move forward from cell to cell.

Personal Expenses	Estimate	Actual
Food	425	435
Entertainment	100	150
Transportation/Gas	50	55
Cell Phone	75	85

9. **Save** ![save icon] the file and leave it **open** for the next exercise.

5.2 Inserting Tables

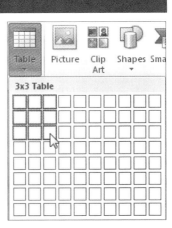

Video Lesson labyrinthelab.com/videos

You can insert a table using the Table ![icon] button on the Insert tab of the Ribbon. The Table button displays a grid that lets you specify the number of columns and rows for your table by dragging over the cells in the grid. The new table is inserted in the document wherever the insertion point is located.

You can also insert a table using the Insert Table dialog box found on the Tables menu in the Insert group of the Ribbon. You choose various options in the dialog box for the table. Also on the Tables drop-down list is a Quick Table menu from which you can choose predesigned tables such as calendars.

Drawing a Table

When you draw a table, you start by choosing the Draw Table command from the Insert Table menu on the Insert tab of the Ribbon. The mouse pointer changes to a pen shape so you can begin drawing the table. First, you draw a simple rectangle. Once you have the overall size of the table, you click and drag inside the rectangle to draw the lines for the rows and columns.

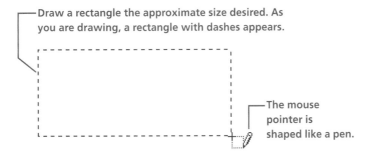

Draw a rectangle the approximate size desired. As you are drawing, a rectangle with dashes appears.

The mouse pointer is shaped like a pen.

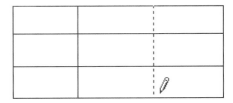

Using the same drag method with the pen shape, you draw the row and column lines at the desired locations.

Although you can choose the number of rows for the table before you enter the data, it is not absolutely necessary to do so, since tapping the [Tab] key in the last cell will add a new row to the table.

Task	Procedure
Insert a table	■ Choose Insert→Tables→Table from the Ribbon. ■ Drag in the grid to select the desired number of columns and rows.
Insert a table using the Insert Table dialog box	■ Choose Insert→Tables→Insert Table from the Ribbon. ■ Set the number of rows and number of columns. ■ Click OK.
Insert a quick table	■ Choose Insert→Tables→Insert Table from the Ribbon. ■ Choose the desired quick table.
Draw a table	■ Choose Insert→Tables→Draw Table from the Ribbon. ■ Click and drag to draw a rectangle for the table. ■ Drag to draw the row and column lines inside the rectangle.

DEVELOP YOUR SKILLS 5.2.1

Insert a Table

In this exercise, you will create a table with three columns and three rows. You will also add additional rows to the table.

1. Position the **insertion point** at the end of the *Schedule Planning* heading on page 3 and **tap** [Enter].

2. Choose **Insert→Tables→Table** [ ] from the Ribbon.

3. Follow these steps to create a three-column, three-row table:

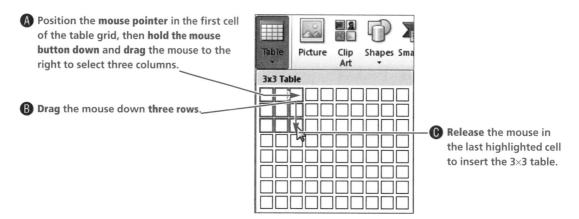

Ⓐ Position the **mouse pointer** in the first cell of the table grid, then **hold the mouse button down** and **drag** the mouse to the right to select three columns.

Ⓑ **Drag** the mouse down **three rows.**

Ⓒ **Release** the mouse in the last highlighted cell to insert the 3×3 table.

4. Position the **insertion point** in the first cell of the table.

5. **Enter** the information shown in the following table using ⎡Tab⎤ to move to the next cell and to add new rows as required.

Course	Days	Units
Math	MWF	3
Science	MWF	3
International Tourism	TTH	2
Biology	TH	3
Biology Lab	W	1

Remember, when you tap ⎡Tab⎤ *in the last cell of a table, Word automatically adds an additional row to the table.*

Copy the Heading Format

6. **Scroll** up to page 1 to **select** *Expense Table* and choose **Home→Clipboard→Format Painter** to activate the tool and copy the selected formatting.

7. **Select** *Schedule Planning* to apply the copied formatting to the heading.

8. **Save** 🖫 the file and leave it **open** for the next exercise.

5.3 Using Table Tools

Video Lesson   labyrinthelab.com/videos

Table Tools consist of tabs on the Ribbon that are *contextual*, meaning they appear in context with the task you are performing. They are comprised of the Design tab and the Layout tab. In order to display the tabs, the insertion point must be inside a table.

Exploring the Layout and Design Tabs

The contextual Layout tab under Table Tools contains command groups associated with the layout (structure) as opposed to the design (attractiveness) of a table. For example, layout options include the following: changing the alignment, inserting and deleting columns or rows, inserting formulas, converting text to tables, and sorting table contents. The Design tab under Table Tools offers commands that include table styles, shading and borders, and other style options.

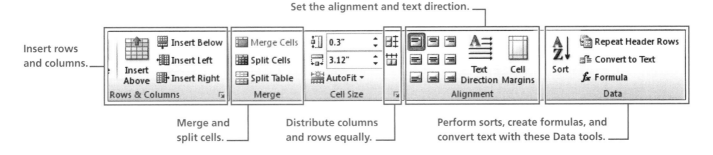

5.4 Converting Tables

Table conversions include converting text to a table or an existing table to regular text. Tabs and spaces are commonly used as separators, such as a tab or a space, between words. One advantage to converting text to a table is the formatting options. For example, in a table, you can add borders around each cell; you cannot do that with text typed in a columnar layout using the ⌷Tab⌷ key.

Converting Text to a Table

The Convert Text to Table command is found in the Tables group on the Insert tab of the Ribbon; if no text is selected, the command will not be active. One of the most common types of text-to-table conversions uses typed text that is currently laid out in a columnar fashion separated with tabs. When you convert, you are telling Word to replace each tab with a new table column.

There must only be one tab character between each column for the conversion to work properly; thus, turn on the Show/Hide formatting marks prior to converting and remove any extra tabs.

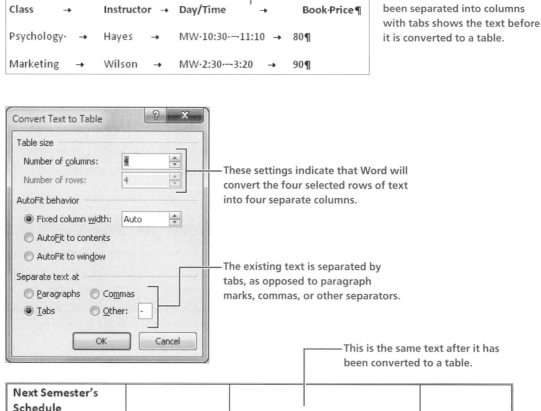

This example of text that has been separated into columns with tabs shows the text before it is converted to a table.

These settings indicate that Word will convert the four selected rows of text into four separate columns.

The existing text is separated by tabs, as opposed to paragraph marks, commas, or other separators.

This is the same text after it has been converted to a table.

Next Semester's Schedule			
Class	Instructor	Day/Time	Book Price
Psychology	Hayes	MW 10:30 – 11:10	80
Marketing	Wilson	MW 2:30 – 3:20	90

Converting a Table to Text

Just like converting text to a table, you can have Word convert an existing table to regular text. You can specify whether the text should be separated by a space or a tab. The Convert to Text command is on the Layout tab under Table Tools on the Ribbon and is only visible when the insertion point is inside a table.

The insertion point must be in the table; however, you do not have to select anything in the table in order to convert it to regular text.

The default for separation is Tabs; however, you can choose other separators here. ——

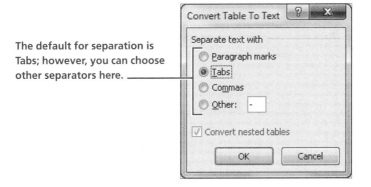

QUICK REFERENCE	CONVERTING TEXT TO TABLES AND TABLES TO TEXT
Task	**Procedure**
Convert text to a table	▪ Turn on paragraph formatting marks, if necessary.
	▪ Ensure there is only one tab separating the columns in all rows.
	▪ Select all lines to be converted.
	▪ Choose Insert→Tables→Table→Convert Text to Table.
	▪ Choose the desired text separator and the number of columns.
	▪ Click OK.
Convert a table to text	▪ Click in any cell of a table.
	▪ Choose Table Tools→Layout→Data→Convert to Text.
	▪ Choose the desired text separator.
	▪ Click OK.

DEVELOP YOUR SKILLS 5.4.1
Convert Text to a Table

In this exercise, you will convert text that is currently in a columnar format, separated by tabs, into a table. For extra practice, you will also convert the table back to regular text.

Convert Text to a Table

1. **Scroll** to the top of page 2 in the document.

2. Choose **Home→Paragraph→Show/Hide** ¶ from the Ribbon.
   You may leave the formatting marks displayed for the entire lesson, or you may turn them off at any time.

3. Position the **mouse pointer** in the left margin next to the *Next Semester's Schedule* heading and then **drag down** to select the lines through *Tennis*.

4. Choose **Insert→Tables→Table→Convert Text to Table** to open the Convert Text to Table dialog box.

5. Follow these steps to create a table from the selected text:

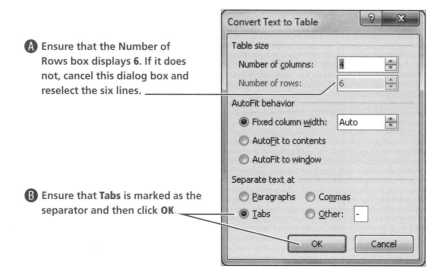

Ⓐ Ensure that the Number of Rows box displays **6**. If it does not, cancel this dialog box and reselect the six lines.

Ⓑ Ensure that **Tabs** is marked as the separator and then click **OK**.

Notice that the text is now in a table with four equal-width columns. Don't worry about the Next Semester's Schedule *heading being in just one cell. You will fix this problem a little later.*

Convert a Table to Text

6. **Click** in any cell in the table.

7. Choose **Table Tools→Layout→Data→Convert to Text**.

8. Verify that **Tabs** is chosen and then click **OK**.
The table is converted back to regular text separated by tabs.

9. Click **Undo** ↻ to return the text to the table format.

5.5 Selecting Data in a Table

Video Lesson labyrinthelab.com/videos

The shape of the mouse pointer changes depending upon whether you are selecting a cell, row, column, the entire table, or certain text within a cell. Each cell contains its own small left margin area. You use the cell's margin to select one or more cells in a row rather than the entire row; the same is true for selecting cells in a column. The following figures illustrate the various pointer shapes that appear when you select different parts of a table.

Point in the margin area of a cell until the mouse pointer changes to a right-tilting, black arrow and then click to select one cell or drag to select multiple cells.

Position the mouse pointer at the top of a column, outside the table, until it becomes a down-pointing, black arrow and then click to select one column or drag to select multiple columns.

Position the mouse pointer just outside the table in the left margin until it becomes a right-tilting, white arrow and then click to select one row or drag to select multiple rows.

Click the square move handle in the upper-left corner of the table to select the entire table. The mouse pointer must be in the table for the handle to appear.

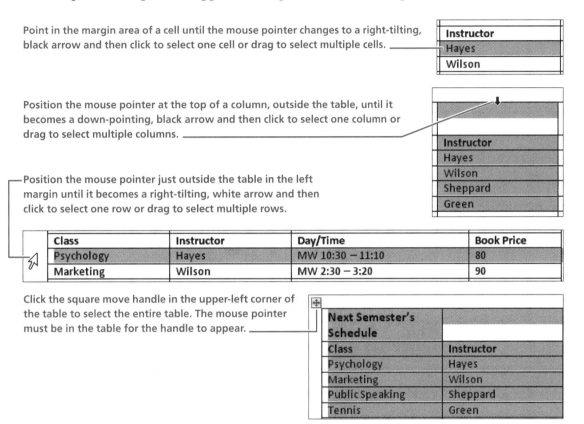

The column widths appear different from what you see on your screen. This is because they have been resized. You will resize your columns a little later in this lesson.

5.6 Aligning Data in a Table

Data can be aligned horizontally or vertically within cells. You can also change the direction of the text within the cells. These commands are found in the Alignment group on the Layout tab when the insertion point is positioned inside a table.

These buttons align data in cells horizontally (left, center, or right) or vertically (top, middle, or bottom).

Use this button to change the direction of text within a cell from horizontal to vertical.

Changing the Text Direction

The default text direction is horizontal. In some instances, you may want the column headings to be vertical with the text facing to the left or to the right. Switching the text to vertical can save space if the table has many columns. The cell height increases automatically to accommodate the change. The same alignment options are available whether the text is vertical or horizontal.

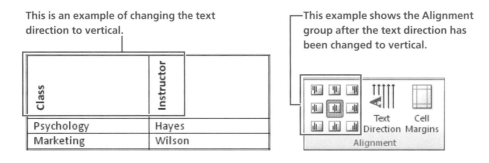

This is an example of changing the text direction to vertical.

This example shows the Alignment group after the text direction has been changed to vertical.

DEVELOP YOUR SKILLS 5.6.1
Select and Align Table Data

In this exercise, you will center-align column headings, right-align the Day/Time and Book Price data, and change the text direction.

1. Follow these steps to select and center the heading's row:

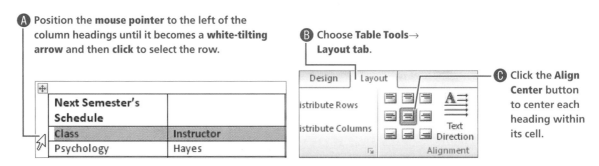

Ⓐ Position the **mouse pointer** to the left of the column headings until it becomes a **white-tilting arrow** and then **click** to select the row.

Ⓑ Choose **Table Tools→ Layout tab**.

Ⓒ Click the **Align Center** button to center each heading within its cell.

2. Follow these steps to select the *Day/Time* and *Book Price* data cells:

Ⓐ Position the **mouse pointer** in the left margin area of the first data cell in the *Day/Time* column.

Ⓑ **Press and hold** the mouse button down, **drag diagonally** to the last *Book Price* number, and then **release** the mouse button.

Day/Time	Book Price
MW 10:30 − 11:10	80
MW 2:30 − 3:20	90
T Th 10:15 − 11:05	35
W 3:40 − 4:30	45

3. Choose **Layout→Alignment→Align Center Right** 📧 from the Ribbon.
   Notice how the data is now lined up evenly on the right side of each cell.

4. **Scroll** up to view the Expense Table and then **select** all the number cells in the Estimate and Actual columns.

5. Choose **Layout→Alignment→Align Center Right** 📧 from the Ribbon.

Change the Text Direction

6. **Select** the column heading row.

7. Choose **Layout→Alignment→Text Direction** 📇 twice to change the direction to vertical, with the text facing to the right.
   Notice how the row increases in height automatically to accommodate the vertical text.

8. Click **Undo** 🔄 twice to change back to the horizontal alignment.
   The row height is also reversed back to the normal text height.

9. **Save** 💾 the file and leave it **open** for the next exercise.

5.7 Merging and Splitting Cells

Video Lesson labyrinthelab.com/videos

The Merge Cells ▦ button in the Layout→Merge group on the Ribbon lets you merge any rectangular block of table cells. Merged cells behave as one large cell. This option is often used to center a heading across the top of a table. You merge cells by selecting the desired cells and then clicking the Merge Cells button.

The Split Cells ▦ button in the Layout→Merge group on the Ribbon lets you split one cell into multiple cells. You can split a merged cell or a cell that has never been merged. A dialog box appears when you click the Split Cells button, which lets you specify the number of columns and rows to create from the split cell.

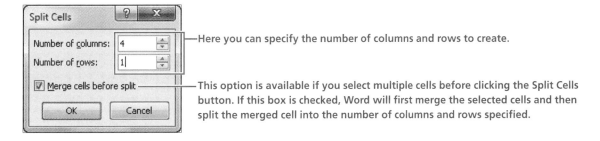

—Here you can specify the number of columns and rows to create.

—This option is available if you select multiple cells before clicking the Split Cells button. If this box is checked, Word will first merge the selected cells and then split the merged cell into the number of columns and rows specified.

DEVELOP YOUR SKILLS 5.7.1

Merge and Split Cells in a Table

In this exercise, you will merge the cells in the first row to create one cell, where you will center the title across the width of the table. Finally, you will convert the title to regular text.

1. Scroll to **page 2**.

2. Follow these steps to merge the first row of the Next Semester's Schedule tab into one cell and center the title:

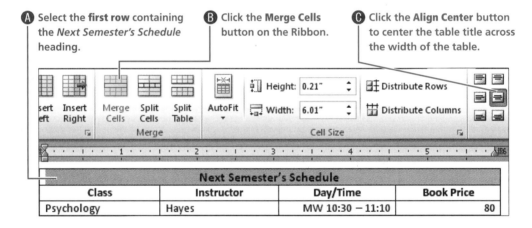

A Select the **first row** containing the *Next Semester's Schedule* heading.

B Click the **Merge Cells** button on the Ribbon.

C Click the **Align Center** button to center the table title across the width of the table.

Next Semester's Schedule			
Class	**Instructor**	**Day/Time**	**Book Price**
Psychology	Hayes	MW 10:30 – 11:10	80

3. With the first row still selected, choose **Layout→Data→Convert to Text**.

4. Verify that *Paragraph marks* is chosen and then click **OK**.
   The title is now regular text and is no longer part of the table.

5. **Save** 💾 the file, and leave it **open** for the next exercise.

5.8 Adding Borders and Shading to a Table

Video Lesson   labyrinthelab.com/videos

You can apply borders and shading to a table through the Borders and Shading dialog box. Alternatively, you can use the Shading and Borders drop-down lists in the Table Styles group on the Design tab. These buttons are interesting to work with because they have a memory. They remember the last option you chose from their menus during the current Word session, and they reflect that option on the button face. This allows you to apply the same formatting multiple times, just by clicking the button face repeatedly rather than opening the menu each time.

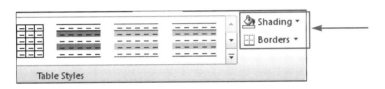

DEVELOP YOUR SKILLS 5.8.1
Work with Borders and Shading

In this exercise, you will remove all borders from your table, and then you will reapply the borders. Finally, you will add shading to your heading row.

1. Click the **move handle** in the upper-left corner of the table to select the entire table. Remember, the mouse pointer must be in the table for the move handle to appear.

Class	Instructor	Day/Time	Book Price
Psychology	Hayes	MW 10:30 − 11:10	80
Marketing	Wilson	MW 2:30 − 3:20	90
Public Speaking	Sheppard	T Th 10:15 − 11:05	35
Tennis	Green	W 3:40 − 4:30	45

2. Choose **Design→Table Styles→** [Borders ▾] **menu ▾** from the Ribbon.

3. Choose **No Border** from the drop-down menu.
   This removes borders from the table. Notice that the button face reflects the No Border icon. Now you'll reapply borders to the table.

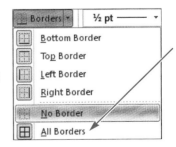

4. Make sure the table is still selected, and then click the **Borders menu ▾** again, and then choose **All Borders** from the menu.

Format the Heading Rows

5. Select the **first row** of the table.

6. Choose **Design→Table Styles→** 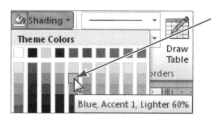 **Shading ▾** **menu ▼** from the Ribbon.

7. Choose the shading color in the **fifth column**, **third row**, Blue, Accent 1, Lighter 60%, as shown at right.

8. **Save** 💾 your document, and leave it **open** for the next topic.

5.9 Sorting Data in a Table

Video Lesson   labyrinthelab.com/videos

The Sort 🔤 button in the Data group on the Layout tab opens the Sort dialog box, which provides options to sort one or more columns in ascending or descending order and choose whether the first row of the table contains column headings. You can choose to sort a table by up to three levels. For example, say you have a table containing column headings for city, state, and zip. You can have Word sort the table first by state, then by city within state, then by zip code within city, for a three-level sort.

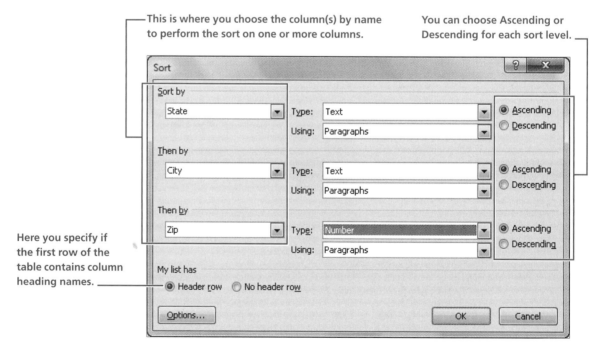

This is where you choose the column(s) by name to perform the sort on one or more columns.

You can choose Ascending or Descending for each sort level.

Here you specify if the first row of the table contains column heading names.

 If the first row contains column headings and you do not specify that the table has a *Header row*, then *Column A, Column B,* and *Column C* will display in the Sort By boxes. When you perform the sort, the actual heading names will be sorted along with the data.

Task	Procedure
Sort a table	■ Click in the table.
	■ Choose Layout→Data→Sort $\begin{smallmatrix}A\\Z\end{smallmatrix}↓$ from the Ribbon.
	■ Under My List Has, choose Header Row or No Header Row.
	■ Under Sort By, select the column or field you want to sort by.
	■ For a two-level sort, under the first Then By, choose the column or field you want to sort by.
	■ For a three-level sort, under the second Then By, choose the column or field you want to sort by.
	■ Choose the Type of information being sorted.
	■ Choose Ascending or Descending for each sort level.
	■ Click OK.

DEVELOP YOUR SKILLS 5.9.1

Sort Table Rows

In this exercise, you will practice sorting the Next Semester's Schedule table.

1. Position the **insertion point** in any cell in the Next Semester's Schedule table.

2. Choose **Layout→Data→Sort** $\begin{smallmatrix}A\\Z\end{smallmatrix}↓$ from the Ribbon.
   Word displays the Sort dialog box.

3. Follow these steps to sort the table:

Ⓐ If necessary, choose **Header Row** to indicate that the first row of the table is a header. This prevents Word from sorting the header row with the other data rows.

Ⓑ This drop-down list originally included column headings titled Column 1 through Column 4. Specifying that the table has a header row caused Word to place the heading names in the list. Choose **Book Price** from the list.

Ⓒ Word automatically sensed the data Type as **Number**.

Ⓓ Leave this option at the default of **Ascending**.

Ⓔ Click **OK** to execute the sort.

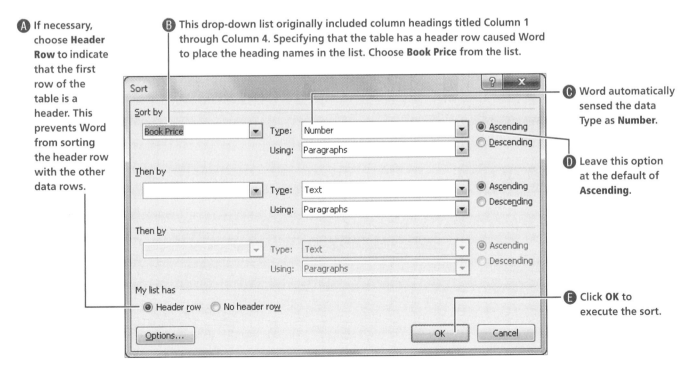

Notice that Word sorts the table rows based on the Book Price column and that now the entire table is selected.

4. Choose **Layout→Data→Sort** $\begin{smallmatrix}A\\Z\end{smallmatrix}\downarrow$ from the Ribbon again.

5. When the Sort dialog box appears, once again make sure **Header Row** is chosen in the bottom-left corner of the dialog box.

6. Choose **Class** from the Sort By list in the upper-left corner of the dialog box, and keep the **Ascending** option as it is.

7. Click **OK** to sort the table.
   Your table is now sorted in ascending order by Class.

8. **Save** 💾 the document, and leave it **open** for the next exercise.

5.10 Inserting Rows and Columns

| Video Lesson | labyrinthelab.com/videos |

You can insert columns to the left or right of existing columns and insert rows above or below existing rows. If you wish to insert multiple columns or rows, you must first select the same number of existing columns or rows you wish to insert. For example, to insert two new rows, you must select two existing rows. You can use the buttons on the Ribbon in the Rows & Columns group on the Layout tab to insert columns and rows, or you can use the drop-down menu that appears when you right-click a selected column or row.

Moving Rows and Columns

You can move a row or column by using the Cut and Paste commands or by using the mouse to drag and drop. When you select the entire row or column and move it to another location, Word automatically makes room for the selection by moving the other rows down or the other columns to the right. However, if you only select the individual cells within a row or column, when you paste, Word replaces any existing information in the cells. You can prevent data loss by inserting a blank row or column prior to moving.

QUICK REFERENCE	WORKING WITH COLUMNS AND ROWS
Task	**Procedure**
Insert rows	▪ Click in the desired row or select the same number of rows that you wish to insert.
	▪ Choose Layout→Rows & Columns.
	▪ Choose either Insert Above or Insert Below.
Insert columns	▪ Click in the desired column or select the same number of columns that you wish to insert.
	▪ Choose Layout→Rows & Columns.
	▪ Choose either Insert Left or Insert Right.

Task	Procedure
Delete rows or columns	■ Select the desired rows or columns. ■ Choose Layout→Rows & Columns→Delete. ■ From the Delete drop-down menu, choose Delete Cells, Delete Columns, Delete Rows, or Delete Table.
Move a row or column using Cut and Paste	■ Select the entire row(s) or column(s) as desired. ■ Choose Home→Clipboard→Cut. *or* ■ Tap Ctrl+x. ■ Select the row to paste the data above. *or* ■ Select the column to paste the data to left of. ■ Choose Home→Clipboard→Paste.
Move a row or column using drag and drop	■ Select the entire row(s) or column(s) as desired. ■ Point the mouse in the first cell and drag to the first cell in the desired row or column (you will see a dotted insertion point that travels with the mouse pointer). ■ Release the mouse button when the dotted insertion point is at the beginning of the first cell in the desired row or column.

DEVELOP YOUR SKILLS 5.10.1

Insert Rows and a Column

In this exercise, you will practice inserting multiple rows and a new column in the table.

Insert Rows

1. Position the **mouse pointer** to the left of the **Marketing** row until it becomes the white-tilting arrow.

2. **Click** and then **drag down** to select the Marketing and Psychology rows.

3. Choose **Layout→Rows & Columns→Insert Above** to insert two new rows above the Marketing row.

4. Add the following data to the new blank rows:

Geometry	Bailey	MW 12 – 12:50	95
Geometry Lab	Johnson	T Th 9:00 – 9:50	35

Insert a Column

5. **Click** in any cell in the first column.

6. Choose **Layout→Rows & Columns→Insert Left** from the Ribbon.
   A new, blank column is inserted at the beginning of the table. Don't worry about the column spacing; you will fix it later.

7. Type **Course #** as the new column heading.

8. **Enter** the following data in the blank column:

Course #
500334
500335
200021
605221
123356
988290

9. **Scroll back up** to the Expense Table on page 1 and then position the **insertion point** in the *Actual* column.

10. Choose **Layout→Rows & Columns→Insert Right** from the Ribbon.

11. Type **Difference** as the new column heading.

12. **Save** the file, and leave it **open** for the next topic.

5.11 Performing Calculations in Tables

Video Lesson   labyrinthelab.com/videos

The Formula dialog box is displayed by choosing Layout→Data→Formula *fx* from the Ribbon. When the dialog box opens, the Formula box displays the Sum function. The Sum function recognizes whether there are figures entered in the cells above or to the left of the formula cell and indicates that in the formula automatically. However, sometimes you may need a formula for something other than adding. In that case, you must use cell addresses in the formula. Although the columns and rows are not lettered or numbered as they are in Excel, you must use *cell addresses* for certain calculations in a table. The first cell in a table is considered to be cell A1 (first column, first row). Word's formulas are not nearly as sophisticated as Excel's; however, they are adequate for simple calculations.

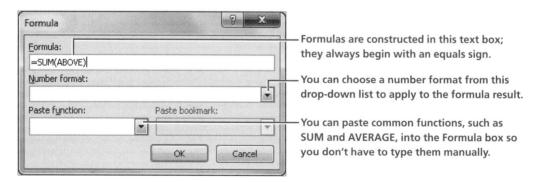

Formulas are constructed in this text box; they always begin with an equals sign.

You can choose a number format from this drop-down list to apply to the formula result.

You can paste common functions, such as SUM and AVERAGE, into the Formula box so you don't have to type them manually.

Constructing Formulas

You construct formulas by typing directly into the Formula dialog box. In Word, formulas can contain a combination of the following elements:

- **Arithmetic operators**—The most common arithmetic operators are + (addition), – (subtraction), / (division), and * (multiplication). For more complex formulas, use Microsoft Excel, then copy and paste the Excel table into the Word document.

- **Cell addresses**—In Word tables, the columns are labeled A, B, C, etc., and the rows are numbered 1, 2, 3, etc. Each cell has an address formed by the column letter and row number. For example, cell A1 refers to the cell in column A and row 1. You can use cell references in formulas. For example, the formula =D2–C2 subtracts the number in cell C2 from the number in cell D2. It is not necessary to type the column letter in uppercase when creating the formula.

- **Functions**—Functions are predefined formulas that perform calculations on cells. The most common functions are SUM, AVERAGE, MIN, and MAX.

  A function is followed by a set of parentheses in which you enter arguments. Arguments include numbers, cell addresses, a range of cells, or direction references (see next bullet). A range of cells is separated by a colon. For example, to include cells C2, C3, and C4 only in a formula, you would type C2:C4.

- **Direction references**—In Word, functions can use direction references to indicate cell ranges. The direction references are ABOVE, BELOW, LEFT, and RIGHT. As an example, the formula =SUM(ABOVE) would sum all numbers above the cell containing the formula.

Word formulas do not recalculate automatically if you change a number in a cell; thus, you must re-create the formula to display the new total.

QUICK REFERENCE	CONSTRUCTING FORMULAS
Task	**Procedure**
Create a formula	- Choose Layout→Data→Formula *fx* from the Ribbon.
	- Delete the formula in the formula box.
	- Type an equals (=) sign.
	- Construct the formula using cell addresses.
	- Use the appropriate operator: + (add), – (subtract), * (multiply), / (divide).
Calculate with a function	- Choose Layout→Data→Formula *fx* from the Ribbon.
	- Delete the formula in the formula box.
	- Type an equals (=) sign.
	- Choose a function from the Paste Function list.
	- Enter the arguments within the parentheses.

Construct Formulas

In this exercise, you will use formulas to calculate the difference for each expense item and then calculate the totals for the Estimate, Actual, and Difference columns.

1. Click in the **Difference** column of the Expense table for the Food row.
   This cell is named D2 because it is the fourth column (D) in the second row (2).

2. Choose **Layout→Data→Formula** *fx* from the Ribbon.

Create a Formula to Subtract the Estimate from the Actual Expense

3. Follow these steps to create a formula to subtract the Estimate from the Actual expense:

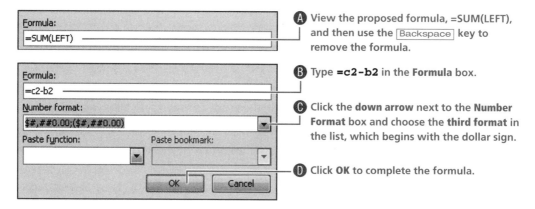

Ⓐ View the proposed formula, =SUM(LEFT), and then use the [Backspace] key to remove the formula.

Ⓑ Type **=c2-b2** in the **Formula** box.

Ⓒ Click the **down arrow** next to the **Number Format** box and choose the **third format** in the list, which begins with the dollar sign.

Ⓓ Click **OK** to complete the formula.

This formula subtracts the estimated food expense (column b, row 2) from the actual food expense (column c, row 2). Notice that the result, $10.00, displays with a dollar sign and two decimal places.

If you wish to display the dollar format without the two decimal places, you must delete them manually from each cell.

4. **Click** in the cell beneath the one with the formula.

5. Choose **Layout→Data→Formula** *fx* from the Ribbon.

6. **Remove** the proposed formula and type **=c3-b3**.

7. Click the **Number Format** drop-down menu ▼ button, choose the format with the **dollar sign**, and click **OK**.

8. **Enter** formulas in the remaining rows in the Difference column.

Create a Formula to Total the Columns

9. Position the **insertion point** in the last cell of the table and **tap** [Tab] to create a new blank row.

10. Type **Totals** in the first cell of the new blank row, and then **tap** [Tab] to move to the next cell in the Totals row.

11. Choose **Layout→Data→Formula** *fx* from the Ribbon.
    Word assumes you want to add the numbers above the formula cell.

12. Click **OK**.

   The result should be 650. Notice that the total does not have the dollar sign or decimals since you did not specify any special formatting.

13. Use the default formula again to calculate the total for *Actual* column with no formatting.

14. Calculate the **total** for the Difference column and add the currency formatting.

15. **Save** 💾 the file, and leave it **open** for the next exercise.

5.12 Sizing Rows and Columns

Video Lesson   labyrinthelab.com/videos

You can easily resize columns and rows in a table. Word 2010 offers a variety of techniques for this.

Dragging to Adjust Row Heights and Column Widths

The adjust ✛ pointer appears whenever you position the mouse pointer on a row or column gridline. You can adjust the column width and row height by dragging the gridline. When you drag a column gridline, the width of the column to the left of the gridline adjusts. When you drag a row gridline, the height of the row above the gridline adjusts. If you adjust the left gridline of the first column, all other columns automatically adjust to accommodate the new width of the first column.

You can adjust the width of the first column by dragging this gridline.

Personal Expenses	Estimate	Actual
Food	425	435
Entertainment	100	150
Transportation/Gas	50	55
Cell Phone	75	85

You can also adjust column width and row height by dragging column and row markers on the ruler.

Double-clicking the border between two columns adjusts the column to the left to *best fit*, meaning the column will be as wide as it needs to be, based on the width of its contents. You can select several columns and double-click to best fit the selected columns all at once.

Distributing Rows and Columns

The Distribute Rows 🗒 and Distribute Columns 🗒 buttons in the Cell Size group of the Layout tab let you equally allocate the space in a table among the rows and columns. For example, if a table is six inches wide and has three columns, the Distribute Columns command will adjust the width of each column to two inches.

Adjust Column Widths

Drag to Adjust Column Width

1. Follow these steps to change the width of the first column:

Ⓐ Position the **mouse pointer** on the border between the first two columns. The mouse pointer changes to the adjust pointer (a double-headed black arrow).

Ⓑ **Drag to the right** about a half inch, and then **release** the mouse button to change the column width.

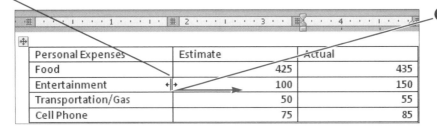

Personal Expenses	Estimate	Actual
Food	425	435
Entertainment	100	150
Transportation/Gas	50	55
Cell Phone	75	85

Notice that the second column is much narrower than the last two columns. You will remedy that right now.

Evenly Distribute Columns and Rows

2. Follow these steps to distribute the last three columns evenly:

Ⓐ Position the **mouse pointer** at the top of the Estimate column until it becomes a **black down arrow**.

Ⓑ **Drag to the right** to select all three columns.

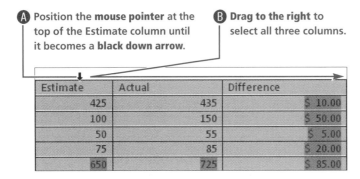

Estimate	Actual	Difference
425	435	$ 10.00
100	150	$ 50.00
50	55	$ 5.00
75	85	$ 20.00
650	725	$ 85.00

3. Choose **Layout→Cell Size→Distribute Columns** 🎛 from the Ribbon to make the selected columns the same size.

4. **Scroll** to the Next Semester's Schedule table on **page 2**.

5. **Select** the entire table and distribute the columns evenly.

Adjust Columns to Their Best Fit

6. **Scroll up** again to the Expense table.

7. Follow these steps to adjust all columns in the Expense table to their best fit:

Ⓐ Click the **square move handle** to select the entire table.

Personal Expenses	Estimate	Actual	Difference
Food	425	435	$ 10.00
Entertainment	100	150	$ 50.00
Transportation/Gas	50	55	$ 5.00
Cell Phone	75	85	$ 20.00
Totals	650	725	$ 85.00

Ⓑ Position the **mouse pointer** on one of the column gridlines until it becomes the adjust pointer and then **double-click**.

All columns are now as wide as they need to be, based on the width of their contents.

8. **Save** 💾 the file, and leave it **open** for the next exercise.

5.13 Using Table Styles to Format a Table

Video Lesson   labyrinthelab.com/videos

The Table Styles group located on the Design tab lets you choose from a variety of predefined table formats. These formats automatically apply borders, shading, font colors, font sizes, and other formats to tables. You may be pleasantly surprised to see the professional-looking formatting that results when you apply Table Styles.

After you apply a Table Style, you can continue to customize the formatting of the table if you wish, adding additional borders, for example.

Checking or unchecking these options determines if special formatting will be applied to specific areas of a table, such as the header row or the total row.

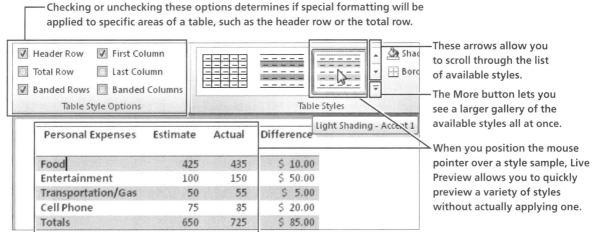

These arrows allow you to scroll through the list of available styles.

The More button lets you see a larger gallery of the available styles all at once.

When you position the mouse pointer over a style sample, Live Preview allows you to quickly preview a variety of styles without actually applying one.

Apply Table Styles

In this exercise, you will add polish to your table by applying one of Word's built-in table styles.

1. Make sure the **insertion point** is in the **Expense** table.

2. Choose **Design→Table Styles** from the Ribbon.

Observe the Table Style Gallery

3. Position the **mouse pointer** in the Table Styles gallery, and move from one style to another. Notice that Live Preview displays how the style would look if applied to your table.

4. Use the **middle scroll arrow**, as shown at right, to scroll down and view other built-in table styles.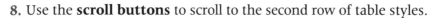

5. Again, use **Live Preview** to examine additional styles.

6. Click the **More** ⊽ button to display a larger sampling of styles, and then scroll through the gallery.

7. **Click** outside the table to close the gallery, and then **click** the table again.

8. Use the **scroll buttons** to scroll to the second row of table styles.

Apply a Table Style

9. If necessary, place a checkmark in the **Header Row** and **First Column** checkboxes in the Table Style Options group, as shown at right, to apply special formatting to those areas of your table. **Check** or **uncheck** the remaining boxes, as shown in the illustration.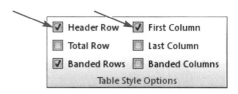

10. Choose the **Light List – Accent 1** style to apply that style to your table.

 The location may vary based on your screen size and resolution. You can use ToolTips to locate the style, or feel free to choose another style.

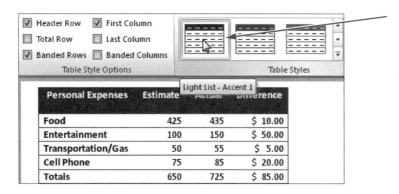

Notice the special formatting on the header row, and notice that bold was applied to the first column. That's the result of options you chose in the Table Style Options group.

Use the Move Handle to Reposition the Table

You used the move handle ⊞ earlier in this lesson to select an entire table. Now you will use it to move your table back to the center of the page.

11. Position the **mouse pointer** over the move handle, and the pointer changes to a four-headed black arrow.

12. **Press** and **hold** the mouse button, **drag** the table to the horizontal center of the page, and then **release** the mouse button.

Adjust Row Height

You've experienced dragging the border of a column to change its width. Now you'll use a similar technique to change row height.

13. Follow these steps to change the height of the first row:

Ⓐ Position the **mouse pointer** on the row border below the first row.

Personal Expenses	Estimate	Actual	Difference
Food		425	435	$ 10.00
Entertainment		100	150	$ 50.00

Ⓑ When the mouse pointer changes to a **double-headed black arrow**, press the mouse button and drag down, until the row is approximately a quarter to a half inch tall, and then release the mouse button.

14. **Select** the first row with the headings.

15. Choose **Layout→Alignment→Align Center**.
    Notice that the text is centered in the middle of the row and the center of each cell.

16. **Save** 🖫 the document, and **close** it.

5.14 Working with Forms

Video Lesson labyrinthelab.com/videos

Many organizations use forms to collect data. Forms contain both fields, where users enter information, and objects such as checkboxes and drop-down lists to assist users with data entry. With Word, you can easily set up forms, based on tables, to meet the needs of your organization and distribute them in any of the following formats:

- **Printed**—Printed forms are printed and filled out on paper.
- **Electronic**—Electronic forms are distributed to Word users and filled out in Word. They are often available via a network or sent in an email.
- **Internet-Based**—Internet-based forms are posted to a website and filled out using a web browser. The data is stored in an electronic database. Word lets you set up forms and save them as web pages.

Address Information				Date Click here to
Name				enter a date.
Address				
City	State	Zip		
How/Where Will You Eat?				
Eat at restaurants ☒	Times per week 0			
Buy groceries and cook ☒	Times p 0			
	1			
Transportation	2			
Use Campus Shuttle ☒	Use ow 3			
	4			
Entertainment	5			
Stay home to watch TV ☒	Times p			
Go out ☒	Times p 6			
	7			

Setting Up Forms

You can set up forms using the same tools and techniques used to set up any other type of document. However, certain Word features are particularly useful with forms. For example, tables are frequently used to set up forms because they allow you to lay out forms with an orderly structure. Creating a form in a table is much easier to work with than using tabs. Word also provides tools in the Controls group on the Developer tab of the Ribbon that can be used to design forms.

DEVELOP YOUR SKILLS 5.14.1

Set Up the Form

In this exercise, you will add a table and custom tab stops to align objects in the form.

1. **Open** the Student Survey document from the Lesson 5 folder.

2. **Select** the title *Georgia South College*.

3. Using the Mini toolbar, change the font size to **16 points**.

4. **Select** *Students Helping Students Response Form*.

5. Choose the **Home→Font→Font Size** 11 ▾ **menu** ▾ button from the Ribbon and choose **14 points** from the menu.

6. Turn on **Bold** **B** and **Italics** *I*.

7. Position the **insertion point** on the line under the subtitle.

Insert a Table

You will use this table as the basis for the form.

8. Choose **Insert→Tables→Table** ⊞ from the Ribbon and select **two columns** and **two rows**.
   You will insert additional rows as needed for the form by using the Tab *key at the end of each row.*

9. Select the entire table and choose **Table Tools→Layout→Alignment→Cell Margins** and change the Top and Bottom to **.08"**.

10. Position the **mouse pointer** on the line between the two columns and drag it to the **right** to the 5-inch mark on the ruler.
This creates a wide first column.

11. If necessary, click the **Show/Hide** ¶ button to turn on the formatting marks.
Seeing the formatting marks makes it easier for you to see exactly what you are doing in the form.

12. Follow these steps to begin adding text to the form.

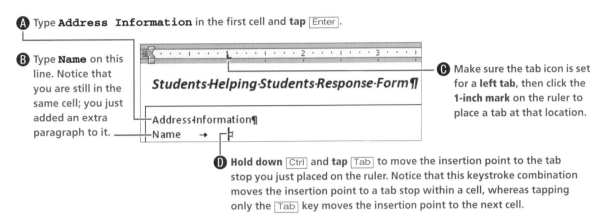

Ⓐ Type **Address Information** in the first cell and **tap** Enter.

Ⓑ Type **Name** on this line. Notice that you are still in the same cell; you just added an extra paragraph to it.

Ⓒ Make sure the tab icon is set for a **left tab**, then click the **1-inch mark** on the ruler to place a tab at that location.

Ⓓ **Hold down** Ctrl and **tap** Tab to move the insertion point to the tab stop you just placed on the ruler. Notice that this keystroke combination moves the insertion point to a tab stop within a cell, whereas tapping only the Tab key moves the insertion point to the next cell.

13. **Save** 💾 the document and leave it **open** to continue with the next topic.

Understanding Form Fields

Video Lesson labyrinthelab.com/videos

Fields in a form are made up of controls. There are three types of controls you can use in a form: content controls, legacy forms, and ActiveX controls. The type of document you are creating and who will be using it determine which control set to use in the form. See the following table for descriptions of each type of control.

FORM CONTROLS	
Type	**Description**
Content Controls	These controls were introduced in Word 2007. The group contains additional controls that did not exist in the legacy tools. However, these do not work with Word 2003 and older versions of the application. They also have limitations on data restriction properties. For example, you can insert a Plain Text Content Control but there is not an option to limit the maximum length for the entry.
Legacy Forms	This older set of form fields is still available. This set does not include the newer controls, such as the Date Picker and Picture controls, but these fields can be used in any Word version and allow data restrictions to be set.
ActiveX Controls	This set of controls is reserved for documents that will be used in a web page.

Using the Form

After you create the form, you should protect it to prevent anyone from making changes to it. You do this by setting a protection that only allows the users to fill in the form. When a protected form is opened, the first form field is highlighted, ready to receive data. Then, you use Tab and Shift + Tab to move to the next or previous field. In this lesson, you will use a combination of content controls and legacy forms form fields for practice.

When you mix control types in a form, you lose some functionality. For example, you have to click in the field, rather than use the Tab key, when moving from a content control to a legacy form field.

The Developer Tab

All three types of controls are found in the Controls group on the Developer tab of the Ribbon. The Developer tab does not appear on the Ribbon by default. You must activate it by placing a checkmark next to *Developer* in the Word Options dialog box. You can open the Word Options dialog box using the File tab or by right-clicking any tab or command on the Ribbon and choosing Customize the Ribbon. Once you turn it on, the Developer tab remains visible unless you uncheck the option or reinstall Microsoft Office.

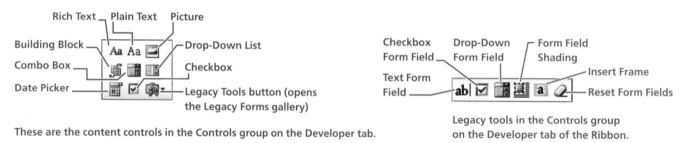

These are the content controls in the Controls group on the Developer tab.

Legacy tools in the Controls group on the Developer tab of the Ribbon.

QUICK REFERENCE	INSERTING FORM FIELDS
Task	**Procedure**
Insert a content control in a form	▪ Choose Developer→Controls. ▪ Choose the desired content control to insert.
Insert a form field from the Legacy Tools	▪ Choose Developer→Controls→Legacy Tools. ▪ Click the desired form field to insert it in a document.

Insert Form Fields

In this exercise, you will display the Developer tab on the Ribbon. You will then use a combination of content control and legacy forms controls to insert text fields, checkboxes, and drop-down form fields in your document.

Display the Developer Tab

1. **Right-click** the Home tab and choose **Customize the Ribbon**.

2. Place a checkmark in the **Developer** checkbox, as shown here.

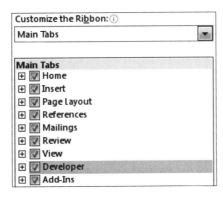

3. Click **OK** to display the Developer tab on the Ribbon.

4. If necessary, click the **Show/Hide** ¶ button to turn on the formatting marks.

Insert a Legacy Forms Text Form Field

5. Position the **insertion point** at the 1-inch tab stop in the first cell of the second row.

6. Choose **Developer→Controls→Legacy Tools→Text Form Field** 𝐚𝐛| from the Ribbon.
   If formatting marks and shading are turned on, the Legacy Text Form Field control will display little circles in a shaded cell, indicating that it is a form field.

7. If a shaded box is not visible, follow these steps; otherwise, go to the next step.
   ■ Choose **Developer→Controls→Legacy Tools** 🦟 from the Ribbon.
   ■ Click the **Form Field Shading** 🄰 button to display the shaded field.
   You won't actually enter data in the fields until the form is complete and has been protected. When you eventually enter data, the length of the text field increases to accommodate the text you type, unless you restrict the field length with property settings.

Insert Additional Text Form Fields

8. If necessary, click to the right of the field, **tap** Enter, and type **Address**.
   Notice that a custom tab stop is set at the 1" position on the ruler. Custom tab stops are paragraph formats, so they are carried to new paragraphs when you tap Enter.

9. **Press** Ctrl + Tab, and choose **Developer→Controls→Legacy Tools** 🦟 from the Ribbon.

10. Click the **Text Form Field** 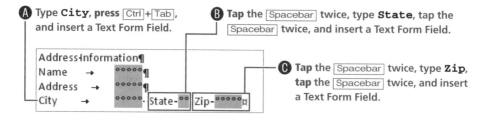 button to insert another text field, and then **tap** [Enter].

11. Follow these steps to insert the text fields for City, State, and Zip:

Ⓐ Type **City**, press [Ctrl]+[Tab], and insert a Text Form Field.

Ⓑ Tap the [Spacebar] twice, type **State**, tap the [Spacebar] twice, and insert a Text Form Field.

Ⓒ Tap the [Spacebar] twice, type **Zip**, tap the [Spacebar] twice, and insert a Text Form Field.

Address·Information¶
Name   →   °°°°°¶
Address →   °°°°°¶
City   →   °°°°°·State-°° Zip-°°°°°¤

Insert a Text Form Field for the Date

12. **Tap** the [Tab] key to move the insertion point to the next table cell on the right.

13. Choose **Home→Paragraph→Align Text Right** ≣ from the Ribbon to position the insertion point at the right side of the cell.

14. Type **Date** and **tap** the [Spacebar] twice.

15. Choose **Developer→Controls→Date Picker Content Control** 🖩 from the Ribbon.

16. Follow these steps to insert the current date into the form:

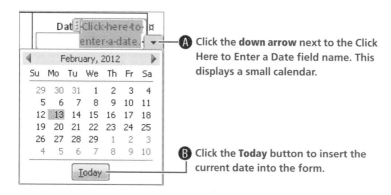

Ⓐ Click the **down arrow** next to the Click Here to Enter a Date field name. This displays a small calendar.

Ⓑ Click the **Today** button to insert the current date into the form.

17. **Save** 💾 the file, and leave it **open** for the next exercise.

Using the Checkbox and Drop-Down List Fields

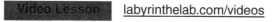 Video Lesson   labyrinthelab.com/videos

In addition to a Text Form Field, Word provides a Checkbox Form Field and a Drop-Down List Form Field. These fields make it easy for users to respond to survey questions and simplify data analysis for the form's creator. Drop-down fields, for example, allow you to enter specific choices to be displayed in a list, while checkboxes restrict answers to a yes/no type of response. You can choose the default entries for each field you place on a form.

How/where will you eat?			
Eat at restaurant	☒	Times per week	0 ±
Buy groceries and cook	☒	Times p	0
			1
Transportation			2
Use Campus Shuttle	☐	Use ow	3
			4
Entertainment			
Stay home to watch TV	☒	Times p	5
Go out	☒	Times p	6
			7

These are checkboxes. The options are to check the box for Yes or leave it unchecked for No. You can choose the default.

This is an example of a drop-down list. You create this list by entering the text that will display when you click the drop-down arrow.

DEVELOP YOUR SKILLS 5.14.3

Add Checkboxes and Drop-Down Lists to the Form

In this exercise, you will continue adding form fields to the document, including checkboxes and drop-down lists.

1. Position the **insertion point** in the first cell of the second row.

2. **Drag** the 1-inch tab stop off the ruler.

3. Place **left tab stops** at the 2-inch, 3-inch and 4.25-inch positions on the ruler.

4. Type **How/Where Will You Eat?**, tap ⟨Enter⟩, and type **Eat at restaurants**.

5. Follow these steps to insert information in row 2:

Ⓐ Remember to use ⟨Ctrl⟩+⟨Tab⟩ between the labels and the form fields.

Ⓑ Place Check Box Form Fields here. Be sure to use the checkbox form field in Legacy Tools.

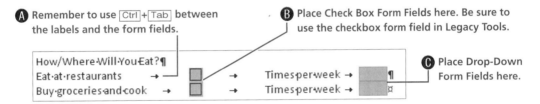

Ⓒ Place Drop-Down Form Fields here.

At this point, nothing happens to these form fields if you click them. They do not become active until you restrict and protect the document as a form, which you will do a little later in this lesson.

6. **Tap** ⟨Tab⟩ twice to move the insertion point to the first cell in the third row.
   Notice the new row maintains the same custom tab stops you placed in the previous row.

7. Use these guidelines to insert labels and checkboxes in the last two rows of the form, as shown in the illustration:

- **Type** the text and insert checkboxes as shown.
- Insert **Legacy Forms** drop-down form fields for the *Times Per Week* data.
- Use Ctrl + Tab between labels and form fields.
- **Tap** Tab to move between cells.

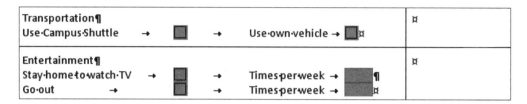

8. **Save** the changes and leave the form **open** for the next exercise.

Applying Field Properties

Video Lesson   labyrinthelab.com/videos

Each field type has various properties associated with it. For example, you can restrict the type and set the maximum length for data entered in text fields. You can also limit users to entering only dates in a field specified as a Date type, and you can have Word automatically format it to a particular date format. Although you cannot prevent all errors during data entry, property restrictions help in that effort.

Modifying Text in a Content Control

The default text is displayed in a content control; for example, the following illustration shows the default text, *Click here to enter text*. This text is replaced when the user selects it and types data in the form. To modify the default text that displays in a content control, you must be in Design Mode. Once in Design Mode, you drag over the text and type the replacement.

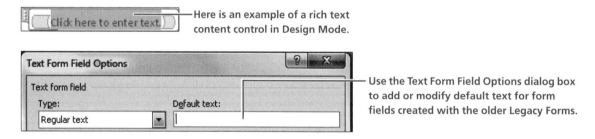

To display and edit text in a legacy control, you must open the Text Form Field Options dialog box and enter or modify the text in the Default Text box. The user must select the default text before entering the actual data in the form.

Task	Procedure
Set properties for content controls	▪ Select the field. ▪ Choose Developer→Controls→Properties from the Ribbon.
Modify text in a content control	▪ Select the field. ▪ Choose Developer→Controls→Design Mode from the Ribbon.
Set field properties for legacy form fields	▪ Select the field. ▪ Choose Developer→Controls→Properties from the Ribbon. *or* ▪ Double-click the form field. ▪ When the Form Field Options dialog box appears, make the desired choices.

DEVELOP YOUR SKILLS 5.14.4
Set Field Properties

In this exercise, you will set field properties for the various field types.

1. Follow these steps to add default instructional text to the Name field:

A **Double-click** the Name field to open the Text Form Field Options dialog box.

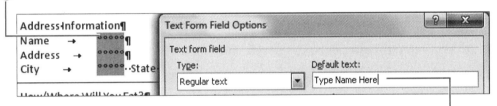

B Make sure the insertion point is in the Default Text box and type **Type Name Here**.

2. Click **OK** to accept the default text and close the dialog box.

3. Click the **Date** field at the top of the right column.

4. Choose **Developer→Controls→Properties** from the Ribbon.

5. Choose the **d-mmm-yy** format from the Display the Date Like This list, as shown here.

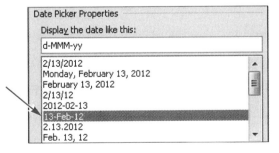

After you specify the date format, when you type a date in the field, Word will apply this specific format.

6. Click **OK** to complete the property settings, then click **Undo** 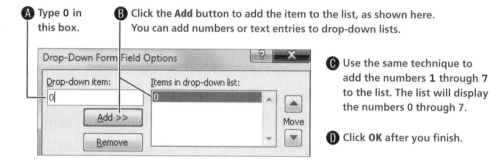 to return to the default format.

7. **Double-click** the State field, set Maximum Length to **2**, choose Uppercase from the Text Format list, and click **OK**.
   This forces users to enter the state abbreviations.

8. **Double-click** the Zip field, set the Maximum Length to **10**, and click **OK**.

Set Drop-Down List Properties

9. **Double-click** the *Times per week* field for the *Eat at restaurants* line.

10. Follow these steps to specify the list items:

Ⓐ Type 0 in this box.

Ⓑ Click the **Add** button to add the item to the list, as shown here. You can add numbers or text entries to drop-down lists.

Ⓒ Use the same technique to add the numbers **1** through **7** to the list. The list will display the numbers 0 through 7.

Ⓓ Click **OK** after you finish.

11. **Double-click** the field next to *Times per week* on the *Buy groceries and cook* line.

12. Using the same technique as **step 10**, specify 0 through 7 in the drop-down list for the other *Times per week* fields.

Complete the Form Design

13. **Select** the table, and choose **Home→Paragraph→Borders** menu ▾ from the Ribbon and choose **Inside Borders**.

14. If necessary, click the **Show/Hide** ¶ button to turn off the formatting marks.

15. If necessary, choose **Developer→Controls→Legacy Tools→Form Field Shading** to turn off field shading.

16. **Save** the changes, and continue with the next topic.

Protecting Forms

Video Lesson   labyrinthelab.com/videos

The Restrict Editing feature can prevent users from making changes other than in the form fields. Protecting forms also triggers the form fields to behave like form fields. For example, tapping the ⌈Tab⌉ key will move the insertion point to the next form field, and clicking a checkbox will insert or remove an X. You unprotect a form when designing or modifying it, and you protect it when you are ready to use it.

Task	Procedure
Protect a form	■ Choose Developer→Protect→Restrict Editing from the Ribbon.
	■ In the Restrict Formatting and Editing task pane, check the Allow Only This Type of Editing in the Document checkbox.
	■ Choose Filling in Forms from the drop-down list.
	■ Click the Yes, Start Enforcing Protection button.
	■ Add and confirm a password, and click OK to use password protection. Otherwise, leave the password fields blank, and click OK to dismiss the dialog box.
Stop protection	■ Click the Stop Protection button in the Restrict Formatting and Editing task pane.
	■ Enter a password if prompted to do so, and then click OK.

Distributing and Using Forms

You can simply print and distribute paper forms to users. Electronic forms should be protected, and they are typically distributed via email. Users can fill out an electronic form online and return the completed form to the person responsible for collecting the data.

Protect and Use the Form

In this exercise, you will protect the form and then enter data in the special form fields you inserted in the document.

Protect and Save the Form

1. Choose **Developer→Protect→Restrict Editing** 📄 from the Ribbon.
   The Restrict Formatting and Editing task pane opens.

2. Follow these steps to protect the form:

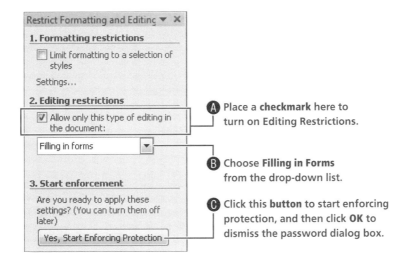

Ⓐ Place a **checkmark** here to turn on Editing Restrictions.

Ⓑ Choose **Filling in Forms** from the drop-down list.

Ⓒ Click this **button** to start enforcing protection, and then click **OK** to dismiss the password dialog box.

3. **Tap** the Tab key three times to move the insertion point from one field to another.

4. **Tap** Shift + Tab to move backwards through the fields to the Name field.

Fill Out the Form

5. Type **Eugene Washington**, and then **tap** the ⌈Tab⌉ key.

6. Type **5250 Ramiro Avenue**, and **tap** the ⌈Tab⌉ key.

7. Type **Richmond,** and **tap** the ⌈Tab⌉ key.

8. Try entering **California** in the State field, **tap** ⌈Tab⌉, and notice that Word restricts the number of characters to two and automatically changed them to uppercase letters.
   This is because you set the maximum field length property of this field to 2 and the text format property to Uppercase.

9. Type **94803** in the Zip field.

10. **Tap** ⌈Tab⌉, click the drop-down arrow in the **Date Picker**, and click the **Today** button in the small calendar.

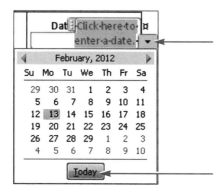

11. Follow these steps to complete the next row:

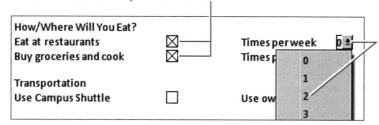

A **Click** the *Eat at restaurants* and *Buy groceries and cook* checkboxes to place Xs in them.

B **Click** the first *Times per week* drop-down field and choose **2** from the list; then repeat for the second *Times per week* in this row and choose **5**.

12. Finish filling in the form as shown in the illustration.

Transportation			
Use Campus Shuttle	☐	Use own vehicle	☒
Entertainment			
Stay home to watch TV	☒	Times per week	5
Go out	☒	Times per week	2

13. **Save** 🖫 the changes, **close** the document, and then **close** the Restrict Formatting and Editing task pane.

14. Reopen the document and then try **clicking** on the title at the top of the form or on any of the text headings.
Word does not respond. When a form is protected, you can only position the insertion point in fields. Also, notice that the text form field next to Name *is now highlighted and ready for text to be entered because it is the first form field to fill in.*

5.15 Concepts Review

Concepts Review   labyrinthelab.com/word10

To check your knowledge of the key concepts introduced in this lesson, complete the Concepts Review quiz by going to the URL listed above. If your classroom is using Labyrinth eLab, you may complete the Concepts Review quiz from within your eLab course.

Reinforce Your Skills

Convert Text, Format, and Sort a Table

In this exercise, you will convert text to a table, apply a table style, and merge cells. Finally, you will perform a multilevel sort, sorting by Last Name, then State.

1. **Open** the rs-Contractors document from the Lesson 05 folder.

2. Beginning with the title, *Independent Contractors for Fast Track*, **select** all of the lines through Steven Johns.

3. Convert the selected lines of text to a **table**, separating text at tabs.
   (Hint: Use Insert→Tables→Table from the Ribbon.)

Apply a Table Style and Merge Cells

4. Use the **scroll down** button in the Table Styles group to scroll down to the fourth row and apply the **Medium Shading 1 - Accent 4** style. The location may vary. If necessary, use ToolTips to locate the style or choose a different style of your choice.

5. Uncheck the **First Column** checkbox in the Table Style Options group on the Layout tab.

6. Use the **Layout→Merge** group to merge the title row, *Independent Contractors for Fast Track*, into one large cell.

7. **Center** the title in the first row.

Sort Rows

8. **Select** the table rows beginning with the column heading. (Do not select the first row containing the table title.)

9. Choose **Layout→Data→Sort** ⬚ from the Ribbon.

10. Specify that the selection contains a **Header Row**.

11. Choose **Last Name** and then **State** for the sort keys, leaving both set on **Ascending**.

12. Click **OK** and examine the results to verify that the table sorted as you specified in step 11.

13. **Save** ⬚ the document and then **close** it.

Independent Contractors for Fast Track					
First Name	Last Name	Rate	Availability	Phone	State
Teresa	Beach	$40/hour	Immediate	213-235-9988	CA
Janet	Bester	$30/hour	April 21	804-450-9090	VA
Julie	Carroll	$35/hour	April 15	510-236-0090	CA
Steven	Johns	$55/hour	Immediate	510-234-8980	CA
Pat	Thomas	$40/hour	May 1	954-223-4565	FL

Format a Table and Use Calculations

In this exercise, you will format the table at the end of the exercise. You will decrease the width of the first three columns and increase the width of the last column. You will also create formulas in a total row.

1. **Open** the rs-Auto Parts document from the Lesson 05 folder.

Format the Table

2. **Select** the first row, and use the **Mini toolbar** to apply bold and center alignment formatting.

3. Select the **second column** by clicking just above the top border of the column when the mouse pointer is a down-pointing black arrow.

4. Use the **Mini toolbar** to center the data in the column.

5. Select the **number cells** in the third column.

6. Choose **Layout→Alignment→Align Top Right** 🔲 from the Ribbon

7. Select the **first three columns**.

8. **Double-click** the border between two of the selected columns to best fit the contents within the columns.

9. Position the **mouse pointer** on the right border of the table. When the mouse pointer changes to a double-headed black arrow, **drag to the right** until the right edge of the table is at the **5 ¹/₂-inch mark** on the ruler.

Use Formulas in the Table

10. Add a **new row** to the bottom of the table and type **Total** in the first cell.

11. Use `Tab` to move to the next cell in the last row.

12. Choose **Layout→Data→Formula** 𝑓𝑥 from the Ribbon.
    The formula in the Formula dialog box automatically defaults to the Function SUM(ABOVE).

13. Leave the formula as is, and click **OK** to insert the formula in the cell.

14. Use `Tab` to move to the next cell, and click the **Formula** 𝑓𝑥 button again.

15. Leave the formula at **SUM(ABOVE)**, and choose the third **number format** from the drop-down list.

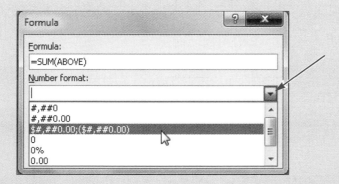

16. Click **OK** to insert the formula.

17. **Double-click** the column border on the right side of the **Cost** column to widen it.

Apply a Table Style

18. Make sure the **insertion point** is in the table.

19. Choose **Design→Table Styles** from the Ribbon.

20. Apply the **third style** in the first row of the gallery—Light Shading, Accent 1—or choose a different table style.

21. In the Table Style Options group on the Design tab, if necessary, check **Header Row, First Column**, and **Banded Rows**. Remove any other checkmarks.

22. **Save** and **close** the file.

Item	Quantity	Cost	Description
Oil Pump	20	$78.20	Lubricates the engine by pumping motor oil.
Oil Filter	20	4.95	Cleans the oil as it circulates through the engine.
Battery	10	45.00	Provides electric current to start the engine.
Starter	10	150.00	Receives energy from the battery, and turns the crankshaft to start the engine.
Muffler	30	79.00	Muffles the sound produced by the engine.
Radiator	5	230.00	Holds and cools the antifreeze.
Total	95	$ 587.15	

REINFORCE YOUR SKILLS 5.3

Insert Fields in a Form

In this exercise, you will create an electronic discount voucher form that fits on a postcard. This provides for an easy mailing campaign.

Set Up the Margins and Paper Size

1. Start a **new** document.

2. Choose **Page Layout→Page Setup→Orientation** 📄 from the Ribbon, and then choose **Landscape** from the menu.

3. Choose **Page Layout→Page Setup→Margins** 🔲 from the Ribbon, and then choose **Narrow** from the gallery to apply 0.5 margins.

4. Choose **Page Layout→Page Setup→Size** 📄 from the Ribbon, and choose **More Paper Sizes** at the bottom of the gallery.

5. In the Paper tab, set the page width to **5"** and the height to **3"**, and then click **OK** to close the dialog box.

6. Choose **Home→Paragraph→Line and Paragraph Spacing** from the Ribbon, set the line spacing to **1.0**, and remove the after-paragraph spacing.

7. Type **TrainRight Discount Voucher** and **tap** ⌷Enter⌷.

Add a Table

8. Choose **Insert→Tables→Table** ▦ from the Ribbon, and insert a **two-column, two-row** table.

9. **Click** below the table, and type **Return card by August 15 to receive discount credit!**

10. Choose **Home→Paragraph→Center** ≡ from the Ribbon to center the line below the table.

11. Select the **title** on the first line, format the text as **Calibri 12 pt bold**, and apply the text **color** of your choice.

12. Choose **Home→Paragraph→Center** ≡ from the Ribbon to center the heading.

Insert Text and Fields

13. Select the table, and choose **Home→Paragraph** from the Ribbon.

14. Click the **dialog box launcher** in the bottom-right corner of the Paragraph group.
The Paragraph dialog box appears.

15. In the **Spacing** portion of the Indents and Spacing tab, replace the 0 with a **3** in the Before spacing box, and click **OK**.
This will create a little extra space between paragraphs as you enter text and fields in the table.

16. Select the **entire table**, if necessary, and set the font size to **9 pt**.

17. Set a left tab stop at the ¼ **mark** on the ruler in the first cell.

18. **Type** text and insert **legacy form fields** in the table cells, as shown in the following illustration. The fields in the first table cell are checkbox fields. Use ⌈Ctrl⌉+⌈Tab⌉ after each checkbox and then type the entry. The Credit Card Type field is a drop-down list field. All fields in the right column of the table are text fields. Use two spaces between labels and form fields except for the checkboxes.

19. **Save** 💾 the file as **rs-Voucher** in the Lesson 05 folder, and leave it **open** for the next exercise.
The form looks ready for use, but it won't be until you protect it in the next exercise.

Set Properties for Form Fields

In this exercise, you will set the field properties for the form fields you inserted in the previous exercise. You will also format the table and protect the form.

Before you begin: Be sure to complete Reinforce Your Skills 5.3. The rs-Voucher document should be open.

Set Field Properties

1. **Double-click** the Credit Card Type field.
   The Drop-Down Form Options dialog box opens.

2. Add the following items to create the drop-down list and then click **OK**: **Visa**, **Mastercard**, **Discover**, and **American Express**.

3. **Double-click** the State field, set the maximum length to **2**, and set the text format to **Uppercase**.

4. Set the maximum length of the **Zip** field to **10**.

Format the Table

5. Reduce the width of the first column by approximately ¹/₂ **inch** by dragging the border between the two columns.

6. Select the entire table, and **remove all borders**.

Protect and Save the Form

7. Choose **Developer→Protect→Restrict Editing** 🔒 from the Ribbon.

8. Follow these steps to protect the form:

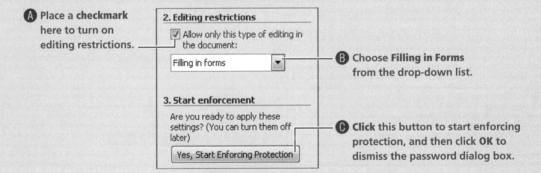

Ⓐ Place a **checkmark** here to turn on editing restrictions.

2. Editing restrictions
☑ Allow only this type of editing in the document:
Filling in forms ▼

Ⓑ Choose **Filling in Forms** from the drop-down list.

3. Start enforcement
Are you ready to apply these settings? (You can turn them off later)
Yes, Start Enforcing Protection

Ⓒ **Click** this button to start enforcing protection, and then click **OK** to dismiss the password dialog box.

Use the Form

Now that you've protected it, the form is ready for use.

9. Complete the form, as shown in the following illustration.

10. Click the **File** tab and choose **Save As**, save the file as **rs-Final Voucher** in your Lesson 05 folder, and then **close** it.

Apply Your Skills

Create a Table with No Borders and Align Data

In this exercise, you will convert text to a table and format it to resemble the table at the end of the exercise.

1. **Open** the as-Word Versions document from the Lesson 05 folder.

2. Use these guidelines to create the following table:
   - **Convert** the text to a table separated by tabs.
   - **Remove all borders** from the table, then **center-align** all of the entries.
   - Apply a **table style** of your choice.
   - **Bold** the first row and apply a **shading** color of your choice.
   - If necessary, use the move handle to **center** the table horizontally on the page.

Company	Word Version	Contact
BPI	Word 2007	David Katz
Exxon	Word 2003	Maria Velasquez
City of Oakland	Word 2003	Michael Gunn
Centron	Word 2007	Ralph Watson
Constructo	Word 2002	Ben Johnson

3. **Save** and **close** the file.

Create Formulas and Format a Table

In this exercise, you will format a table, align data, merge cells, and enter a formula.

1. Follow these guidelines to format the table shown at the end of this exercise.
   - **Open** the as-Order Tracking document from the Lesson 05 folder.
   - Adjust all columns to their **best fit**.
   - **Merge** the cells in the first row.
   - Type **Total Orders** in the first cell of the last row, and place a **formula** in the last cell of the last row to **total** the numbers in the last column.
   - **Align** the data as shown in the example.
   - **Center-align** the table on the page using the **move handle**.

Order Tracking Sheet				
Customer ID	Order Status	Item #	In Stock?	Order Total
233	I	S230	Y	$23.45
234	S	A321	Y	$45.87
341	S	A423	Y	$100.91
567	I	S345	N	$43.23
879	H	D567	N	$78.92
Total Orders				$ 292.38

2. **Save** and **close** the file.

Create an Electronic Form

In this exercise, you will create an electronic form that includes text fields, checkboxes, and drop-down lists.

1. If necessary, start a **new** document.

2. Set the page orientation to **Landscape**, the paper width to **7 inches**, the paper height to **5 inches**, and all four margins to **0.75 inch**.

3. Insert a table with **two columns** and **eight rows**.

4. Set the top and bottom cell margins to **0.05"**.

5. Use these guidelines to set up the form shown at the end of this exercise:

   ■ Set **tabs** at suitable locations for the social security number, driver's license number, and the three investment objectives.

   ■ Enter the items in the **table rows** as shown, using appropriate spacing between labels and fields.

   ■ Insert **legacy form fields** as shown. The Investment Experience and Risk Tolerance fields should use drop-down lists. Use the list entries **Little**, **Moderate**, and **Extensive** for the Investment Experience list. Use the list entries **Conservative**, **Moderate**, and **Aggressive** for the Risk Tolerance list. Use the Date Picker content control for the Date field. All other fields are either text fields or checkbox fields.

   ■ Set the maximum field length of the State field to **2** (formatted as Uppercase), the Zip field to **10**, the Social Security Number field to **11**, and the Driver's License Number field to **8**.

   ■ Format the Annual Income and Net Worth fields with a **Number** type and a **Currency** number format.

   ■ Choose **Design→Table Styles** from the Ribbon; apply the **table style** of your choice from the Table Styles gallery.

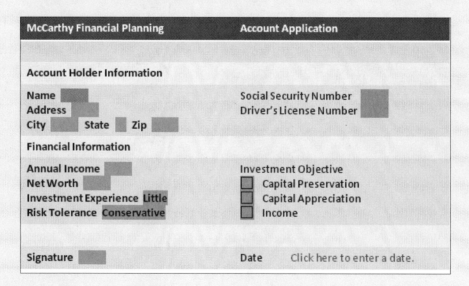

6. **Protect** the form without using a password.

7. **Save** the form as **as-McCarthy** in the Lesson 05 folder.

Critical Thinking & Work-Readiness Skills

In the course of working through the following Microsoft Office-based Critical Thinking exercises, you will also be utilizing various work-readiness skills, some of which are listed next to each exercise. Go to labyrinthelab.com/ workreadiness to learn more about the work-readiness skills.

5.1 Create a Product Comparison Matrix

WORK-READINESS SKILLS APPLIED

- Serving clients/ customers
- Solving problems
- Thinking creatively

Bethanie has been asked to create a product comparison matrix highlighting the differences between My Virtual Campus and their leading competitor, University LAN (U-LAN). Open a new document. Start with a 3×3 table (add rows as needed). Type **My Virtual Campus** and **U-LAN** as the headings for each of the last two columns. Create a list of features (make them up) down the first column and indicate with a **yes** or **no** if My Virtual Campus or U-LAN includes that feature. For example, you may indicate that My Virtual Campus supports video chat while U-LAN does not. Format the table as you see fit to make it attractive yet easy to read. Save the file to your Lesson 05 folder as **ct-Product Matrix**.

5.2 Create a Form

WORK-READINESS SKILLS APPLIED

- Serving clients/ customers
- Thinking creatively
- Participating as a member of a team

Bethanie has been asked to create a customer survey form. If applicable, work with a partner to brainstorm a list of questions to ask, such as name, email address, college, date, favorite My Virtual Campus feature, etc. Create a table to help lay out your questions and then create the form fields that will allow users to easily answer the questions. At a minimum, use plain text, a drop-down list, the date picker, and checkbox controls. Use other controls as necessary. Format the table and form so it is easy to use. Save the file to your Lesson 05 folder as **ct-Survey Form**.

5.3 Modify a Form

WORK-READINESS SKILLS APPLIED

- Participating as a member of a team
- Thinking creatively
- Exercising leadership

Start with the ct-Survey Form you created in the previous exercise. Insert a new top row, merge the cells, and type a title for the form. Save the form to your Lesson 05 folder with the new name **ct-Form Final**. Exchange forms with a partner and test each others' forms. Offer constructive suggestions for improvement. Based on your partner's feedback, modify your form. Rearrange the form fields, change the formatting, add or remove a question, etc. Save your changes.

Index

Notes

Notes